The Entrepreneurs Guide to Building Irresistible Landing Pages

How to Reach a Wider Audience, Get More Leads, and Skyrocket Business Revenue

By Daniel Ndukwu

Copyright Information

Copyright © 2017 by Daniel Ndukwu

This book or any portion thereof may not be reproduced or used in any manner whatsoever without the express written permission of the publisher except for the use of brief quotations in a book review or blog post.

First Published, 2017

The name, copyright, and logos of various companies used in this book are the sole property of those companies and is **not authorized by, sponsored by, or associated with the trademark owner.**

All Rights Reserved.

https://www.iaexperiment.com

All information in this book is purely for educational purposes and should in no way be taken as qualified financial or legal advice. Please speak to your legal advisor or financial consultant before making important decisions.

Table of Contents

The Entrepreneurs Guide to Building Irresistible Landing Pages

   How to Reach a Wider Audience, Get More Leads, and Skyrocket Business Revenue

Copyright Information

Table of Contents

Dedication

   Social Media

Introduction

Chapter One: The Power of Landing Pages

   What is a Landing Page and why do you Need Them

   Benefits of Landing Pages

Chapter Two: The Essential Metrics to Watch on Landing Pages

   Conversion rate

   Cost per action or Cost per sale

   Abandonment Rate

   Your One Metric

Chapter Three : Landing Page Killers and What to do About Them

   Not Focused

   Sucky Headline

   Too Many Elements

   Too Many Offers

   Overall Aesthetics or the Normal Site Design

   Being Lazy

Chapter Four: Essential Elements of Your Landing Pages

- Attention Grabbing Headline
- Graphics/images
- Compelling Copy
- Privacy policy and TOS
- Social proof that actually matters
- Benefits vs features
- Let's talk about fake benefits for a moment
- Features Vs Benefits
- Real Benefits Connect Desires
- The offer
- Clear Call to action

Chapter Five: Landing Page Rules

- One page one goal
- Only essential imagery
- Use only real authority
- Whitespace is king
- Tweak load times
- Keep interest and add value
- Don't exaggerate but still rave
- Test everything

Chapter Six: Writing Hypnotic Landing Pages

- Start with the end goal
- Everything has only one job
- Audience Awareness
- Message match to USP

- Less is more
- Use you – have a conversation
- Long copy if it's necessary – keep the copy tight
- Use bullets points
- Keep paragraphs short
- F-type Landing page design
- Let your customers write it for you

Chapter Seven: Choosing the Right Software
- Lead Pages
- Unbounce
- Instapages
- Instabuilder 2.0

Chapter Eight: The AIDA Formula
- Attention
- Interest
- Desire
- Action

Chapter Nine: Making Money with Thank you Pages
- The Thank You Page

Final thoughts on Building Irresistible Landing Pages

Urgent Plea!

Dedication

This one is for my family. They've supported me through all my harebrained schemes, now it's my turn.

Social Media

Connect with me on Twitter

https://twitter.com/daniel_ndukwu

I'm also active on Quora

https://www.quora.com/profile/daniel-ndukwu

Meet me at The Experiment

https://www.iaexperiment.com/

Introduction

I've been building websites since I came of age. It started with HTML websites. You had to upload the webpages through a client and if you made a mistake it was a bitch to find the cause. After that, we moved onto WordPress affiliate sites that made money through the Clickbank network. Now I've got everything from Shopify stores to dedicated websites where I sell information.

Throughout it all, I've been building landing pages. Some of them were beautiful but converted almost no one. Some of them were hideous and pulled thousands of leads and dollars. Back then, it was pretty hit and miss.

I'd more or less copy something I thought was working, spend a small fortune driving traffic to the page, and cross my fingers. As I've said, it was pretty hit and miss.

After a while, I figured there must be something more to the equation. Like any self-respecting entrepreneur, I decided to do something about it. I began the long slow process of educating myself at the school of trial and error.

At the time, it was difficult to find solid information and even more difficult to find software dedicated to creating landing pages.

I would learn during the day, build at night, and drive traffic in the morning. Over time, I started to see patterns. If you created a headline in a certain way, it'd generate more leads.

If you set up your offers like so then you'd pull twenty percent more revenue.

As long as you had enough white space, you could get readers to scroll beyond the fold.

Slowly but surely, my conversions moved up and my revenue followed. Now, it's almost like second nature when developing landing pages.

Even though I'm an old hand at it after building hundreds of pages, there's something I want you to do.

Test everything.

My business is unique to me. What works like gangbusters for me may only bring back mediocre results for you. In this book, I've done my best to give you insights that can be applied across all industries. That doesn't mean you should copy and paste them.

You still need to break them down and apply them in the context of your business. If you can do that then you'll be a rockstar when it comes to building high converting landing pages.

By the time you're done reading this book, you'll be creating landing pages for lead generation and sales that blow your old ones out of the water.

To make this entire process even easier for you, I've put together a bunch of resources. They include dozens of headline formulas, a swipe file to get you started, and a landing page checklist. You can access them here https://www.iaexperiment.com/landing-worksheets

Now that we're on the same page, let's jump into the process of building truly irresistible landing pages that convert prospects, build revenue, and establish long term relationships.

P.S. Lest I forget. To get featured across our network of pages, retweeted, or mentioned take a picture of your book with the following hashtags. Or, use the hashtags to give me a shout and let me know you're enjoying it.

#landingpageboss

#LikeABoss

#LikeABossSeries

#TheXPLife

#XPNation

Chapter One: The Power of Landing Pages

In the digital marketing and online business community, landing pages are inviolate. They're the difference between a successful campaign and one that makes you question the results people claim to be getting.

The wrong ones will make the internet spew hate and vitriol then push you into a downward spiral leading to a long, slow, agonizing death.

The right landing pages turn browsers to fans, haters to friends, and customers to advocates. People share them on social media and the world creates hashtags in your honor.

There's a fine line between high performing landing pages and the ones that'll make you wonder if the time you spent on them was worth it.

Old advice like "use red in your headlines" and "create multiple columns on your pages" will kill conversions faster than a prize winning thanksgiving turkey.

Your audience is jaded.

They've been on the web for years. Many of them were born into the web and may know more about it than you.

You're doing yourself, your brand, and your customers a disservice by trying to get away with poorly designed and researched landing pages.

If you're like me a few years ago, you'll think I'm blowing it out of proportion. When I started building landing pages, I'd slap together a headline, body copy, and maybe add an image as an afterthought.

To make it worse, I'd make only one or two landing pages and send all my traffic there no matter what offer they'd seen or what my goals were.

The customer? They came last of course.

Thousands of dollars and hours of frustration forced me to do better.

It's funny, when your pocketbook is at stake, you become wise–fast. Visit my website and you'll encounter landing pages everywhere. If you visit the same page after a few days, you'll see a different version. It's an iterative process

The pages are linked throughout my blog, they show up in search results, and they're in my menu.

Why?

Because I know how powerful they are when used correctly. It's even more pronounced when you don't have much traffic. If your website is receiving a million visitors a month you can disregard this book because you'll get customers and subscribers no matter what you do.

If you're like the rest of us mortals then keep reading. You'll find gems in this book and learn how to create more powerful landing pages that move your business forward.

Before we dive into making the ultimate landing pages, you and I need to be on the same page.

What is a Landing Page and why do you Need Them

Technically, a landing page is the first page a visitor encounters when they get to your website. It can be your about page, your home page, or your blog page.

Any page a visitor can "land" on.

While those pages can and should be optimized for conversions, (especially the about page because it's one of the top three visited pages on a website) they're not what I'm referring to when I say landing page.

Whenever you see "landing pages" in this book, it's referring to dedicated pages made and optimized to do one thing.

That could be to make a sale.

That could be to promote a sign up for a mailing list.

It could also be to promote a giveaway.

Whatever.

The overarching theme with the landing pages I discuss is they have one desired outcome. The rest of the pages on your website have too many distractions. Those include links in the body text, menu buttons, popups, footer links, a sidebar, etc.

Let's redefine landing pages to reflect the focus of this book.

Landing pages are standalone web pages distinct from your main website that has been designed for a single focused objective. This means your landing page shouldn't have global navigation, in text links, or extraneous elements like a sidebar.

There are many types of landing pages.

1. **Click through pages.** These are pages, generally on Ecommerce websites, used to promote clicking through to the next page

where the sale can be made. Think of them as teaser pages which warm up the prospect for the main offer.

Though they're generally used in Ecommerce, they can be adapted to other funnels such as digital products. Daryl from LionZeal.com uses click through pages and storytelling to get an amazing optin rate on his landing pages.

2. **Lead generating pages.** This is the most common type of landing page. Their focus is to get your visitor to part with their contact information so you can market to them later in a more controlled setting EG Email.

    It's done by giving away something of value in exchange for the contact information. A few examples of lead magnets are:
    - Ebooks
    - Webinars
    - Cheat sheets
    - Video tutorials
    - First chapter of a book
    - Free consultations
    - Contests
    - Free trial
    - Notifications on updates
    - Whitepaper

3. **Sales pages.** The most important pages on your website. This is where the money is made and, by its nature, has the lowest conversion rate. On average, Ecommerce sites see a 2%-4% conversion rate and SaaS companies see 3%-5% conversions. Of course, your product or service could be a necessity, novelty, or other –ty that makes it convert much higher.

The goal of this book is to increase conversions across the board and make your business run smoother, grow faster, and crush your goals.

I have a confession. It's hard to start from scratch and build high converting landing pages. You have too many assumptions going in that need to be tested.

What kind of assumptions you ask?

Well, for starters, you assume your headline is good. You assume your button placement is the best one. You assume your offer resonates with your customers. You assume your copy is well written. You assume these and dozens of other things.

Those assumptions should be tested at every turn by data. You observe and react to the data. It doesn't matter what your gut says if the data doesn't back it up.

At times, the process can be tedious and discouraging. I want to let you know the tangible benefits you'll receive as a result of optimized landing page. Look back at this list when you get tired of the optimization process and want to throw in the towel.

It'll always be worth it.

Benefits of Landing Pages

I'm only going to touch on a few of the many benefits of landing pages. There are so many I could write a book on only that.

I digress.

The versatility of landing pages is what makes them so powerful. You can change colors, fonts, images, copy, and anything else you want with just a few keystrokes and button clicks.

Try doing that with the design you paid your developer for. Or what about the marketing videos you're thinking about making. How hard will those be to change?

Anyways, let's move into the most powerful positives of landing pages.

Skyrocket Website Conversions
What if you had a three page website? One page is your homepage. The other page is your about page. The last page is a landing page optimized for sales. You may convert at a few percentage points. More likely, you'll convert at below a percentage point.

What happens when you have dozens of landing pages in addition to the three pages I just mentioned?

You have one for giving away an Ebook. You have another one for a nice tool. Still another one gives away a piece of software. Oh, I forgot the one you have for a free consultation. Together, the dozens of landing pages more than 10x your subscriber conversion rate.

Every subscriber you gain is another opportunity for the sale. With email marketing, you'll blow your normal conversion rate out of the water.

This isn't a book on email marketing, but the two go hand in hand. The increased conversions via landing pages coupled with a strong email marketing campaign will do wonders for your bottom line.

Data gathering and usage behavior
It's the internet of things. We're all connected. Whether that's good for us as individuals is up for debate. There's no denying its good news for your business.

Imagine you're getting poor conversions on your product pages. You drill down into the data and realize most of your visitors are using Chrome and Safari browsers. You also notice you're getting much better conversion rates from visitors using Firefox and Internet Explorer.

You could ignore it, but you dive deeper and realize the difference is statistically significant (that basically means it's not a fluke).

You use an android device and Mozilla Firefox when you access your pages. You've not experienced any issue when browsing.

You forget about it and start doing something else. While you're working, you can't shake the feeling that something's wrong. You can't ignore what you saw, so you borrow your friends IPhone and navigate to your landing page.

The images aren't lining up well, the text is off center, and the page looks like it was dug up from the nineties.

You're stunned.

You download Google Chrome and navigate to the page. The same thing happens. Element aren't where they're supposed to be, your font colors are off, and it looks like a child put the page together.

You're mortified.

How many people saw this page and decided your business sucked? After all, what kind of company can't even put a page together correctly?

You figured out an important piece of information with just one data point. Imagine what you can do when you have multiple data points to compare.

Sure, Google analytics gives you information, but dedicated landing page software gives you the data you need without having to prepare tedious custom reports. I've been there; it's not fun or easy.

This is a more extreme example, but when you have accurate data to work with, you'll begin to understand gaps and see patterns you can exploit.

Better Data Backed Decisions
With better data come better decisions. I talked about the ability to gather data in the last point. Now, I want to talk about what you can do with that data. In business, you need to know your costs and the effectiveness of your distribution channels right?

If a direct mail piece is pulling $500 in profit for every one hundred spent, you'll ramp it up – right?

The same applies to the web. If your Facebook ad campaign is pulling in profits then you'll put more money behind it – right?

Of course.

With the vast amount of data you'll be able to collect like where people came from, which ones became customers, which traffic source bounced, how long they stayed on the page, etc. you'll make better decisions.

How would you change your campaigns if you realized the thousand dollars you spent on Facebook was only bringing in half as much as the thousand you spend on Instagram?

I bet you'd cut your Facebook ad spend and refocus it on Instagram.

Your decisions cease to be made based on how you feel. They become decisions you're confident in. It's no longer "we do it like this because it's always been done like this" to "we do it like this because we've run the tests."

You make better decisions when you have better data. Hold your data inviolate.

Build Hype and Validate Products/Ideas
This is one of my favorite uses of landing pages.

In early 2016, I was throwing around the idea of building a new product. I was pretty sure people needed it. At the same time, I didn't want to spend months creating it then watch it fall flat on its face.

I asked a few people who'd opted in for something similar in the past. They said they were interested. I know how valueless it can be when people tell you they like your idea. When it comes time to buy, they're the first to flee the scene.

Anyways, I decided to set up a landing page to validate the product, collect contact details, and presell.

That's right; I wanted to sell spots for something I hadn't even created.

I set up a basic landing page with a catchy headline (more on that in chapter four), a few bullet points, and a simple offer. The page converted at 17.5% and got me 500 subscribers.

I could've stopped there, but went a step further. I continued the conversation by sending out real emails asking them what resonated with them about the offer, how I could improve it, and any other thoughts they had.

With their feedback, I started working. After a few weeks, I sent them another email asking them if they wanted to prepay for early access and a steep discount. When the dust settled, I had a few thousand dollars in my pocket for a product that didn't exist yet.

It's because I built a landing page first.

You can also use a landing page to build hype. If I knew what I wanted to create right from the beginning, I would've taken a different route. I would've created a page with a countdown timer and description. If you signed up, you would get a certain discount when it went live.

Can you see how versatile landing pages can be?

Create more variety
In my experience, no one likes a one trick horse. It's human nature. No matter how amazing something is the first time, we get tired of it.

How do you think people feel about your product or service? Unless it's a matter of life and death it'll get old.

When Facebook appeared on the scene, it didn't have one tenth of the bells and whistles it does now. It was a place to catch up with friends and follow companies you like. Now, there are ads everywhere, you keep getting requests to play games, and it tracks your movements in the real world.

It's a bit creepy.

Even though we criticize the way Facebook has changed, it wouldn't be here today if it would've stayed the same.

No matter what you're doing or selling, you need to create variety in your business.

If you've had only a few products, landing pages are a way to introduce new products gradually while testing market feedback.

If your blog is playful and laid back, landing pages are an outlet to get down to serious business. It's your choice how you introduce variety. Landing pages just happen to be an amazing vehicle for it.

Cater to more User Segments
This follows on the heels of variety. You may have one or only a few products and not need any more. Even if that's the case, your customers will use your product differently.

Take Pinterest for example.

The main website was built for a certain demographic of people. Those are well to do, educated, and married women. In 2017, men have become the largest growing segment of their user base.

Those are for the users — the buyers. They have another section of their website entirely for advertisers and business owners. These people are the ones who're paying the bills and need resources and tools to make the most out of Pinterest.

It's not limited to marketplace type businesses or social media. Think about a photographer. They take pictures of weddings, birthdays, bar mitzvahs, and everything in between. When someone lands on their website, they want information relating to their specific situation. They don't want the generic spiel.

You can apply the same principle to almost any industry. The financial services sector needs different faces for students, young workers, high net worth individuals, and businesses.

The construction industry builds retail spaces, homes, and multi-unit housing complexes. Do you think those people need the same information? No, they don't. They need content, images, and offers related to their specific situation.

Even if you don't have dozens of products, you have different user segments which have different needs. The more optimized landing pages you have, the more opportunities there are to connect with different market segments.

Improve Marketing Campaigns
One of my biggest pet peeves is clicking on a link for a specific item and being dumped on the homepage. Yes, the homepage may have some of the information I'm looking for, but I have to keep clicking to get the entire story.

Why?

Why would you make me do extra work? Every extra step I have to take is an added layer of resistance. Unless I'm a highly motivated buyer, I'm likely to bounce and never return.

The good news is that most websites are waking up and send individuals to specific landing pages. Not all, but most.

Landing pages improve marketing campaigns because you're able to drill down into the needs of a specific group of people. It can be a campaign which deals with your new vacuum cleaner, but there are different types of people who need it.

You have the single mom, you have the college student, and you have the elderly couple.

For each of these groups, you'll highlight different benefits to the potential customer. For the single mom it could be how affordable and durable it is. For the elderly couple you can touch on how quiet and easy to use it is. You can lead with low maintenance and its chic design when talking to college students (and how cheap it is).

Every marketing campaign and segment within that campaign should have a dedicated landing page. I know that's not always possible for various reasons. Chief of which is data and time, but it's something to strive for when optimizing your pages.

Put List Building on Steroids
This is the most popular use of your landing pages. It's almost as important as using them for sales pages.

 Almost.

The sidebar on your website works, but many people experience blindness. Think about how you personally use websites. Do you give the sidebar more than a passing glance?

No?

Neither does the rest of the world. Most websites don't make it worth your time. They add ugly graphics, uglier optin forms, and the occasional greatest hits collection.

On average, the sidebar conversion rate hovers between 0.5% and 1%. Those are good numbers. Most websites don't achieve that without rigorous testing.

Dedicated landing pages are a different beast. On average, conversion rates climb well into the teens. For every 100 people that visit a landing page created to get contact details, 15-20 of them will become email subscribers.

I'm sure you know as well as I do that email subscribers are the bread and butter of cost effective marketing campaigns.

With an optimized landing page, those numbers can easily double or triple. It's not by accident. By A landing page focuses the attention and gives your prospect two options.

Either they perform your desired action or they exit the page. There aren't a bunch of miscellaneous links for them to click on, no menu buttons, and only one call to action.

Improve Credibility
Last but not least, landing pages improve your credibility in the eyes of your visitors.

Let me explain.

Throughout your website, you have elements scattered about. Maybe you have featured in logos on the about page and homepage.

You also have testimonials on different portions of your website. They work together to let the people visiting know you're credible. In addition to that, you have a great design and other things going for you.

With a landing page, you incorporate those elements into one page.

You have testimonials, featured in logos, and a unique design all on one page. You use persuasive language and pull out the big guns to establish trust.

Instead of someone needing to navigate to your homepage, then your about page, then the testimonials page, and maybe a few blog posts, you do the work for them with a well-designed landing page. It's a shortcut to the credibility needed to make a sale.

In a nutshell, landing pages are an asset. The more you have the greater your conversions across the board. In a 2016 study, it was discovered that conversions went up by 55% once a website had ten or more landing pages.

That means just one landing page won't cut it. Five landing pages won't cut it either. It's a constant process of creation and iteration. Throughout the rest of this book, you're going to be equipped with the insights and strategies to turn your landing pages into works of art.

Artwork that builds your business.

Make sure you get the worksheets that come with a checklist, swipe file, and headline formulas. https://www.iaexperiment.com/landing-worksheets

Chapter Two: The Essential Metrics to Watch on Landing Pages

In the old days there wasn't an accurate way to measure certain types of advertising. They had no accurate ways to track TV or radio ads. The big advertising agencies took advantage of this. They told their clients these campaigns were meant as image builders.

They wove a tale of brand recognition, customer loyalty, and prestige. They were missing one ingredient—sales. Fast forward fifty years and we can measure almost everything. Now, the question is, what do you measure?

Digital marketing and online business can be a doozy. There are different schools of thought when it comes to the right Key Performance Indicators (KPIs). Some people say the amount of traffic you get is inviolate.

Others argue that your social media engagement is the most powerful measure of your businesses health. There are other groups that say comments and shares will tell you everything you need to know.

In my opinion, most of those things are vanity metrics. If you have a million monthly visitors and only fifty become customers, what's the point in all that traffic?

If you have a crazy amount of social media engagement but none of those people visit your website then why does it matter?

If they're sharing your content but don't perform your desired action then something is off. Did you know a large percentage of people who share your articles never visit your website?

I was born with a poor capacity for multitasking. I have an even poorer capacity to hold contrasting views in my head.

On the one end, I'm a diehard believer in the 80/20 rule. 80% of your results will come from 20% of your actions. I've seen this simple principle proven time and time again.

The 80/20 rule is in direct opposition to what many gurus' in my industry tell you. Measure everything. If I measured everything I wouldn't have the time to write this book.

If I measured everything I wouldn't have time to build products and services to grow my business.

If YOU measure everything, you'll start to see what's not there in the data. Don't measure everything. Measure what matters. The next question is "what matters?"

From years of trial and error, I've settled on three metrics that matter more than anything else. Together, these metrics give you the information you need to make the most of your landing pages.

Conversion rate
The first metric and possibly the most important is the conversion rate. It's the number of people who perform your desired action. That could

be a sale, a download, or a free trial. It depends on your business or your goals.

What matters is your desired action has been carried out.

There are a lot of benchmarks floating around the internet so let me throw some out there so you have an idea.

For a retail site like Amazon, the average is 2%-5%. Anything higher than that is considered great. For a lead generating site the average is 15%-20%. Any higher than that and you're in coveted terriroty.

Now, most websites on the internet are performing well below average and that could be for any number of reasons. Maybe their messaging is off (check out my book *Craft Magnetic Marketing Messages)*, the products are poorly priced, or they're vague about what's being offered.

Most people don't convert. A retail website with a 10% conversion rate is leaving 90% of their sales on the table. A lead generating website is leaving 80% of their contacts on the table.

The majority of the web is NOT clicking buy, is NOT responding to your offer, and NOT downloading your awesome lead magnet.

What's going on?

How can you change the status quo?

We'll get into it a bit later, it's fascinating.

For now, let's look at how to manually calculate conversion rate.

Take the number of sales you've had over a given period. Then take the number of visitors over the same period. This information is readily available in your analytics.

Divide the number of sales by the number of total visitors and multiply by 100. That's your conversion rate percentage.

For example, if you've had one thousand visitors over the last seven days and 45 sales you'd divide 45 by 1000.

45/1000 = 0.045.

Your sales conversion rate is 4.5%. If you get two percent or less then you have plenty of room to improve.

With an average order volume of $100 and a conversion rate of 1%, you make $1,000 for every 1,000 visitors. Double your conversion rate to 2% and you're making $2,000 for every one thousand visitors.

You've effectively doubled your income without increasing your traffic.

Do you see why conversion rate is so important?

Cost per action or Cost per sale

CPA or CPS is an important metric. They're slightly different. The cost per action is how much you spend get a single lead, download, free trial, etc.

The cost per sale is how much you spend to get a sale. The number is easy to arrive at.

Take the total advertising cost and divide by the total sale or actions. For example, if you spend $400 on advertising and get 75 leads and 20 sales then your CPA is $4.21.

How did I arrive at that number?

I simply added the number of leads and the number of sales. Those are two different actions performed when we spent $400. I then divided 400 by that number.

To get my cost per sale, I'll repeat the process, but this time I'll only look at the number of sales made and ignore the number of leads I got. The cost per sale in this example is $20.

Now, I know I need to make more than $20 per sale to turn a profit. In reality, you don't need to recoup those expenses on the first sale. Many times, you lose money getting new customers.

For example, I advertise many of my books for free. I spend money to give away a free product. That's because I know my numbers. For every Ebook that's downloaded, I make roughly a dollar. That's irrespective of whether or not it's free.

If I spend $200 and get a thousand downloads, I know I'll recoup my advertising costs over time. It doesn't even have to be from Ebooks. There are multiple touchpoints in any given funnel you can use to sell.

Knowing your CPA and CPS allows you to optimize your landing pages until you either reduce the costs or increase the value.

Abandonment Rate
Ten percent of your visitors leave after landing on the first page of your website. It could be the homepage, a sales page, or a lead capture page.

Whatever.

Most of the time, they constitute unqualified traffic. The people who came to your website accidentally or aren't interested in what you have to offer. You wouldn't have converted them anyway.

The next group of people is the one you need to worry about. They're the ones who're sufficiently interested in what you're offering to click through to another page. 55 percent of your website visitors fall off at this stage.

After the third click, you've lost 80 percent of your visitors. Anyone who stays after that is either interested in your offer or doing market research.

This metric matters because it helps you pinpoint issues and bottlenecks. For example, if you see most of your visitors drop off after visiting the about page, it's safe to assume something is rubbing them the wrong way.

If, after reading your blog post and clicking a few of the calls to action, you notice that one landing page seems to drive away more visitors than others. You've just identified a place you can improve.

The abandonment rate, unlike the other two metrics, isn't stand alone. Its value only becomes apparent when it's used in relation to the other metrics you're tracking.

Your One Metric

Every business is unique. In all my books, blog posts, and products, I shy away from telling you this is the only way something is done. At most, I'll tell you this is how I did it and I'm sure if you can learn and adapt it to your situation, you'll do fine.

I've started a lot of projects in my life. I won't call them businesses because not all of them evolved into that. With each project, there was a metric that was more important to its success than anything else.

With self-publishing, that metric is the number of downloads. I know, from experience, that if x number of people download one of my books, y number will go to my website and x will become a customer.

When I was working on a content website, the most important metric was traffic. We knew that if x people visited the website, we'd make roughly y dollars.

With The Experiment, the most important metric is how many people become email subscribers. I know every email subscriber is worth seven dollars. Every time someone signs up for my mailing list, it'll average out to seven dollars in revenue.

I'm in the process of launching a lifestyle fashion brand. The One Metric for that business will be completely different than The One Metric for my self-publishing business or The Experiment.

It could be average order value. If that's the case, every landing page on the website will be optimized toward increasing that value either directly or indirectly.

Maybe we find out that once people buy from us, no matter how small the sale, 86% buy again. In that case, the most important metric to us is getting the initial order. Everything will be geared towards making that a reality.

What's the most important metric in your business? Doubling this metric would have the largest impact on your life.

Don't worry if you don't know it off the top of your head. It usually takes a bit of trial and error before you know what it is. Some metrics will appear to be Your One Metric, but after a while, you'll find something more important.

You can calculate all of these metrics yourself. There is an easier way. In Chapter Seven, I'll introduce you to some great software for both analytics and landing page creation.

For now, I want you to focus on finding Your One Metric. Sure, you may be lost at first, but eventually, you'll know it. Once you do, actively grow it. Everything else improves with it.

In the next chapter, we're going to switch gears and focus on identifying the mistakes that kill landing pages. They're simple, but can gut you before you've even started. Once we're done identifying the mistakes people make without knowing it, we'll get down to the nitty gritty of building landing pages piece by piece.

If you've not gotten them already, make sure to download the free worksheets which include the landing page checklist, swipe file, and headline formulas.

https://www.iaexperiment.com/landing-worksheets

Chapter Three : Landing Page Killers and What to do About Them

We've covered a bit of ground and still have a lot of work to do. Now that we're on the same page, we can begin your education properly.

If you've been playing up until this point, now's the time to get down to business.

It's always a shame when I see landing pages that've done many things right, but kill conversions because they've also done many things wrong. The mistakes that kill landing pages aren't' glaring.

They're not written on the body.

The mistakes don't shout and beg for you to correct them.

No, that would be too obvious. They require a focused and experienced eye to spot them because on other parts of your website, they'd be considered best practices. You see where the problem lies?

Your landing page can survive almost anything except for the mistakes I'll be outlining in this chapter. If you commit them, you'll see conversion rates plunge, cost per action rise, and abandonment rate skyrocket.

None of those are outcomes we're looking for so let's dive into the mistakes and what to do about them.

Not Focused

The first thing to look at before everything else is whether your landing page is focused or not. Does it convey one message and only that message? Are all the elements you've added to your page moving your prospect closer to the ultimate goal?

If not, scrap them. They're hurting you more than they're helping you. It can be tempting to add a few attention grabbing devices like a pulsing form or a gif. On these pages, less is almost always more.

Devices that make them pause and look break the spell you're weaving.

When I say focus, I'm not talking about the elements on the page. They play a role of course. What I'm talking about is your writing, your prose.

From the very first line to the last line there is one goal, for them to buy what you're selling. Even if it's a lead generating page, you're selling something they have to buy. The price may be in real dollars or it can be as cheap as an email address.

Whatever.

Your job is to be intimately familiar with what you're selling and why they'd want to buy it (if you're at a loss, pick up my book *Craft Magnetic Marketing Messages* in the Kindle Store. It's an in depth guide that focuses on market research and creating messages that resonate with your audience).

Once you understand what they want and how you fill that need, your pages reflect their desires with every line. Right from the headline down to the call to action.

Don't stray from that focus to tell a funny story.

Don't stray from that focus to make a point.

Don't stray from that focus to prove you know what you're talking about.

Don't stray from that focus to highlight research.

You can do that in your blog posts. Your landing page is a different beast entirely.

Respect it.

Sucky Headline

Le old headline. The make or break portion of your page. It's been widely quoted that 5x more people read the headline than the body copy.

Put it to the test yourself. Stroll through your Facebook feed. How many articles and ads do you click on? Yea, just a fraction of headlines you see will be blessed with your click.

We're going to look at how to make mouthwatering headlines in Chapter Four. There are also formulas in the worksheets. If you've not already downloaded them then make sure you do that now.

Anyways, the reason why headlines are so important is because people don't have time. You and I are busy. Online, everything is free so we're not obligated to sit down and listen or read anything.

It's different when you're in college or at work. You're paying or being paid to do what you may not like. You suck it up because it'll pan out in the future.

Online, where is the promise that it'll pan out in the future? The promise is in the headline. The worst ones are vague and uninspired. You can use a psychological phenomenon called curiosity gap to create a vague headline and still get people to click. It's difficult and iffy at best. In other words, it's not the best route to go if you've not been actively practicing the art of headline creation for a while.

We're going to look deeper at this in Chapter Four. For now, keep in mind that you should spend just as much time on a headline as you spend on the body copy.

If you've spent an hour crafting your landing page then you should spend an hour or more crafting your headline.

Too Many Elements
I'm 27. I'm getting old. Not old like my back is about to give out. Old in the sense that I've been on the internet for as long as I can remember.

We grew up with an AOL dial up connection before we moved over to a cable modem. Now, there's Wi-Fi in every McDonalds and Starbucks in America.

I'm tired of the same old landing pages and when I browse, I have at least five tabs open. Any excuse you give me to bounce and I'll take it.

The moment it's difficult for us to find the information we're looking for is the moment we close out the browser tab your landing page lives on.. Everyone I know uses the internet the same way.

Every element you add is another opportunity for distraction to set in. We're already distracted enough when we're online. Your visitor's phone is sending them a dozen Whatsapp messages, Instagram is telling them they've gotten a hundred likes on their last picture, and Twitter is informing them about the latest viral trend.

We can't compete. The last thing you want to do is split their attention even further. That slide in optin form you wanted to incorporate – don't.

That gif you found hilarious? Leave it on the blog.

Those images that tell a story? Let them tell the story someplace else.

The name of the game is attention. Attention is hard to get and harder to keep.

The human brain can only process about 110 bits of information a second. A normal conversation takes about 60 bits of neural processing capacity. That's why it's hard to use your phone and have a meaningful conversation at the same time.

Every element on your landing page takes up a few bits of information above and beyond what they're using to read. Make it easy on your visitors. Allow them to go through the process with as little effort as possible.

They'll thank you and your conversion rate will thank you.

Too Many Offers
Another silent killer is choice. Barry Schwartz, an accomplished psychologist, wrote *The Paradox of Choice* (recommended read) in 2004. It's an eloquent argument about the problems inherent in infinite choice. When we have infinite goals, we never accomplish them all.

To achieve a goal, you have to make a series of choices. Sometimes those goals are small like "I want to buy a new pair of jeans." Even with that, you have hundreds of options.

Sometimes, those goals are life changing like "I want to attend college." With hundreds of options for college bound graduates, the opportunity cost of choosing the wrong school is massive.

In the not too distant past, we didn't have much choice. If you were working class, you could have any jacket you wanted—as long as it was black. Henry Ford was a genius by the way. Now, walk into any clothing store and every color under the sun is represented. I won't get into the different materials which add another layer of complexity.

Schwartz changed the way we think about choice. Choice doesn't make us happier, it makes us more miserable. Every time we make a choice, we're missing out on what we didn't choose. Opportunity cost and buyer remorse is at an all-time high.

The concept hasn't become mainstream and probably never will. The reason is simple. Capitalism thrives on the illusion of choice.

In our consumption focused society, we equate happiness with the ability to choose. The reality is that the more choices we have the more stressed we become. With more stress comes a reduced ability to make meaningful decisions.

I recently bought a pair of boots online. It took me two weeks to research, compare, and finally buy one I was happy with.

Why?

Because I had too many options. All of them looked amazing and were fairly priced. How would I choose the best one? In the end, my partner chose from a list I had prepared. It may seem like I'm an indecisive individual. To an extent that may be true. At the same time, I had too many options. When humans are faced with too many choices, they do nothing.

I did nothing.

There are times when choice is good. You get to choose your career path. You get to choose what you eat for dinner. You get to choose your life partner.

Your landing page isn't one of those situations. The more choices you have, smaller your conversion rate. Your job is to boil it down to a single option. Either they say yes or they say no. You can also give them variations of the same option.

If you've got a big ticket item then you can give them an option for payment plans. What you never want to do is introduce two different offers together. That would be bad.

Overall Aesthetics or the Normal Site Design

Remember in Chapter Two I mentioned how landing pages can add variety to your business and attract different people? Well, part of the way that happens is through the design.

If you're using blogging and content marketing as a lead generation and sales tool then, more than likely, you're using a CMS. WordPress, Drupal, or Blogger are different types of CMS you can use. With CMS come design templates. The premium ones offer a lot of customization and versatility.

The normal layout of your blog posts, with the after post optin, sidebar, and menu are fine throughout most of your website. On landing, they spell disaster.

It causes confusion, promotes distraction, and dilutes your message. Avoid it at all costs.

Being Lazy

The last piece of the landing page killing puzzle is your approach to creation. The effort you put in shows.

Your design, the words you use (and don't use), the presentation, the length, etc. all play a part in the conversion rate of your website. Did you know 80% of your visitors stay above the fold?

The reason why is simple. Most pages don't give their visitors a reason to keep scrolling. In the early days of the internet, web users weren't conversant with the way the internet was laid out. They didn't scroll.

Now, they do scroll, but only if it's worth their time. They'll also read everything you write—if it's worth their time. Make it worth their time by clearly spelling out what you're offering and being clear about the benefits (and upfront about what you're not offering).

Just because you get it doesn't mean everyone else does. I remember I was explaining a concept to one of my clients about email marketing. I thought the information was well known to almost everyone. My client was blown away.

The point is that you have to be clear. Never assume anything. Be excruciatingly detailed and above all stay focused with your message.

These are the main killers of landing pages. There are more mistakes you can make, but they're not fatal. I've mentioned the ones which will kill you without a second thought.

Do I sound pessimistic? Sorry. You can't make the most of your pages if you don't know the biggest obstacles facing you.

The aim of this book is to not only equip you with timeless strategies to create irresistible landing pages, but to give you a foundation on which to grow. You can't grow if you don't know when you've made a mistake.

Although I can't be there to look over the shoulder of every landing page you create, (I can look at some, just shoot us an email with the subject line: **Landing Page Feedback** to support@iaexperiment.com), with this information, you can enlist the help of a friend or colleague to put your pages through the ringer. You'll be happy you did.

In the next chapter, we're going to dive in and dissect the essential elements of landing pages.

If you've not gotten them already, make sure to download the free worksheets which include the landing page checklist, swipe file, and headline formulas.

https://www.iaexperiment.com/landing-worksheets

Chapter Four: Essential Elements of Your Landing Pages

Landing pages come packed with a slew of moving parts. To me, they're the most dynamic parts of your website. Unlike your about page or blog pages which you create and revisit periodically, the landing page is always changing.

You'll be testing and refining them until you're sure they deliver what you need from them. As we've said many times in this book. The goal of your landing page depends on your business and Your One Metric.

This chapter is about the essential elements you'll be using on your landing pages. Some of the elements are necessary no matter what your page is about. Some of them can be left off and still achieve your desired effect.

Most of the time, these elements proceed in a pretty straightforward manner. You've got your headline, your subheadline, your first call to action, a hero image (optional), the body copy, and the rest. At other times, you can mix and match them to your heart's desire.

It's up to you to make that call. After all, it's your business, your goals, and your landing pages. I'm just here to equip you with a strong foundation for everything else.

Before we get started, I want to stress how fluid your pages can be. It all depends on your goal. A sales page is much longer than an email capture page. A free trial page will have a different design focus than a sales page.

Always remember, once you master the rules you can bend and even break them. These are your building blocks, the fundamentals. Learn them and then create something truly unique.

Attention Grabbing Headline

The beginning of your journey is and always will be your headline. This is your promise, your big idea. If it falls flat then no amount of conversion devices will save you.

People tend to give the headline too much work. They want it to capture attention. They want it to deliver a promise. They want it to serve as a call to action. They want it to tap into the desires of their audience. They want it to get them to rank in search engines. The list goes on.

Stop.

Your headline has one job. If you stretch it, you can get away with giving it two jobs. Never more. When you want it to have three or four jobs, it does all of them poorly.

The job of your headline is to keep visitors on the page and read the next line. That's it. Its job is not to sell. Its job is not to rank you for keywords.

Its job is not the million and one other things you've heard a headline can do.

That's not its job.

The subheadline's job is to get your visitors into the body copy with as little friction as possible. Sure, your headline and subheadline can communicate a benefit, but that's a side hustle. The main job is to keep the visitor reading.

Your landing page doesn't exist in a vacuum. Before people got there, they saw an ad, a social media post, a call to action in an email, etc. They have a vague idea about what they're about to get into and are interested.

Your headline's job is to hold that interest long enough for them to get into the body copy. The length of which is determined by their level of awareness. We'll get into that later in Chapter Five. For now, let's look at how to craft headlines.

Do you know Cosmopolitan? It's the magazine. Have you ever seen it on the rack when you're about to checkout at the grocery store? Their headlines are gripping.

Go buy a few magazines and study them. You'll learn a thing or two about writing headlines. Another piece of advice I'll give you is keep a personal swipe file.

Whenever you're browsing the internet, reading a magazine, or flipping through a newspaper, take note of the headlines. Take a picture or screenshot of any one that jumps out at you and save them in a folder labelled swipe file on your desktop.

Any time you're ready to write an awesome headline, review your swipe file to get warmed up.

Many times, a great headline starts with a great formula. These are plug and play devices where you just fill in the blanks and eight times out of ten, you've got an effective headline. I provided quite a few in the worksheets (https://www.iaexperiment.com/landing-worksheets), so I'll only touch on a few here.

1. **Incorporate Psychological Triggers.** We like to think we're advanced and civilized. Normal devices won't work on us because we no longer live in caves and have sex with everything with a hole. That's a lie we tell ourselves to keep our sanity. Sentences starting with high impact words like explosive, scientifically proven, secret, new discovery, etc. spark our interest and focus our attention.

   The Scientifically Proven Method to Lose Weight and Keep it Off.
   Shocking Discovery Reveals Why You've Failed to Lose Weight—It's Not Your Fault
   Rediscovered Secret The Wives of Pharaohs Used to Keep Their Skin Flawless.
   I can go on for days, but you get the point.

2. **Ask a Question.** Questions are the spice of life. With the right questions, you get the right answers. With the right questions, you get the right people interested. Ask a question that speaks directly to the problem you're solving.
   Are you tired of trying every new diet and failing to get results?
   Do you want to kill yourself in the gym for the rest of your life?
   How long will you keep trying diets that just don't work?
   Do you want a scientifically proven method to lose twenty pounds in thirty days?

3. **Lead With the Benefit.** At times, it pays to tell people what they're getting up front. You may have fewer clicks, but the

people who do land on your page are more likely to perform your desired action. For example, if your major promise is more traffic you can lead with "get in the first page of Google's SERPs within 30 days." Most website owners would be keen to figure out how they could do that.

4. **Take a Cue From the News.** There's a reason news headlines are written like [person from place] discovers a new way to [desired outcome] without [challenge associated with desired outcome]. That would look like:
Georgia Man Discovers a New Way to Gain a Six Pack Without Going to the Gym Every Day.

5. **Use "How to" or "How I."** A tried and tested way to create a killer headline is either by showing the viewer they're going to learn something or show them how you do something amazing. If you've strolled around the web for any amount of time then you should be familiar with it.
The Counterintuitive Way I Make Six Figures Selling One Dollar Products.

As an entrepreneur who's in charge of developing landing pages that'll make or break their business, you should test. Test these headline formulas and the ones in the worksheets. Mix and match them like I did in the examples above.

Soon, you'll understand what works best for you and your business. The better you get at writing headlines, the better you'll be at converting prospects into customers.

An example headline and why it works

Prosperity, Passion, Priority, Freedom, and Family.

This is the headline from Ken Evoys Successful Site Building System Business. At first glance, it looks like a bunch of words strung together.

Not much of a headline right? Well, if I was his target market, a 27 year old bachelor, it wouldn't be.

I'm not his target market.

He's focused on married people who're tired of the slog of the nine to five and want another outlet to make a living. The headline stresses benefits for people in his market who want financial success. You'll notice that it doesn't focus on financial success itself.

Most people don't want money because it gives them a warm fuzzy feeling. They want money because of the security and freedom it gives them. This headline shows Ken understands this relationship and what his audience desires.

Graphics/images

Images support your message. They never take away from it. Your images add information when words would be a poor substitute.

People add extraneous images when they're lazy. In normal blog posts and pages, images add relief for the eye. In a world of text, images are welcome relief. Unfortunately, that's not the case with your landing pages. The wrong image only serves to confuse your prospect. It detracts from your message.

Cute puppies, cats, and memes have no place on your landing pages. You're engaging in serious business and no matter how playful your brand is, you can't get away with playing with peoples time, money, or attention.

When in doubt cut it out.

There are a few ways images can help convey your message and focus the attention of the reader on what you have to say. Let's look at those now.

1. **Show them where to look.**

Directional cues have been used in advertising for a while because they work. After a certain age, in almost every society, we learn to follow the gaze of others to alert us to danger or pleasure. Countless studies have been used to prove this fact time and again. On your landing page, preferably above the fold, use an image that points your visitors in the direction of your headline or your call to action.

People work best, but directional cues such as arrows have the same effect.

2. **Let the Image Support Your Headline**

Your headline is the promise. It makes sense that the images and graphics on the page support that promise. At times, your offer may be a bit abstract like a video course. In these cases, you can use a graphic illustration of CDs, books, or a video player.

When your product is more tangible, you can show people using and enjoying it. If you sell clothes, show people that. If you're selling a gym membership then show people having a good time working out.

Your image should never overpower the headline.

3. Emotions

Facts tell but emotions sell. An emotional appeal, used the right way, can almost never go wrong. A thick, guttural, emotional reaction will entice visitors to stay on the page and find out more.

The problem with capturing emotion is that it's difficult. We've each had different experiences. What you may associate with joy may mean something else for another person. With emotions, err on the side of caution.

Joy and happiness are the easiest emotions to convey. In my experience, everything else is a coin toss. Emotions are a coin toss. Use them sparingly.

4. Bold Colors

There's a whole branch of psychology dedicated to colors. Did you know that white is considered the color of mourning in some Asian cultures? Nothing grabs attention like the right colors. You have your brand colors and then you have complimentary colors. Switch it up here and use a color that contrasts sharply with the one's you've chosen for your landing page.

Conversely, you can choose a plain color background that puts more emphasis on the message of your headline and the body copy.

5. Illustrations

Not everyone can get away with illustrations. If your brand lends itself to illustrations then by all means use them. A word of caution: invest in custom images. It's more than a little difficult to find stock illustrations that'll fit your needs.

Always consider who you're serving. The illustrations you use for an older audience will be different from the illustrations you use for a young audience. Make sure your illustration doesn't overpower your message, but rather compliments it and you'll be fine.

6. Hold a mirror to your prospect

We identify with people who are like us. When you know exactly who you're serving, you can show them an image of themselves. Remember we talked about the different segments you can serve?

You can show the different people who use your service on every landing page while adapting the language to fit. If you know your customers are young college students, a hero image of young college students works well to reinforce that.

Compelling Copy

I wish I could give you the nuances of writing amazing copy in a few pages. I can't. It's a lesson I'll dedicate another book to.

Don't worry; in chapter nine, we're going to dive into AIDA (attention, interest, desire, action). For now, let me give you a quick rundown that'll help you instantly improve your copywriting.

   1. **Know Your Customer.**

The last thing you do when writing copy is write. The process starts well before that. In fact, the process starts before you make a product. It begins with the research you compiled about your audience.

What are their needs, wants, and deepest desires? All your copy does is reflect what they already want.

You and I don't create motivation on our websites.

We don't create desire.

We don't create need.

The only thing we do is tap into it.

We channel it.

We amplify the motivations, needs, and desires already present.

You can build on them to create something even more powerful. Even then, you can't create it out of thin air.

Motivations are created by society, marketing, family, friends, PR, propaganda, and many other factors. When you understand those motivations — when you've done the research — you can piggyback off the built up motivation.

Your copy also encompasses how you're going to make them a reality.

You don't write copy. Your customer writes it for you. Do your research.

2. Get rid of slogans and jargon.

Jingles may work on the radio or at three AM when the only people watching TV are the ones lacking a life. For the rest of the world, it's a waste. I was looking through some old advertising spots when I came across the slogan "Don't smoke, it's a matter of life and breath!"

I'm sure the brilliant ad agency that came up with it was paid handsomely. I'm also sure it didn't prevent one person from picking up a cancer stick. Tell me about Johnny Blues who got cancer from smoking. Tell me about Sally Greens who aged prematurely.

Talk to me. Communicate a message.

By the way, it wasn't until those smart folks at the surgeon general's office told young women smoking made them age early that they saw a sharp decline in new and old smokers alike. They told them something they cared about and got their desired results

If you dare use industry leading expert on any of your landing pages I will personally send a billion bots to overload your server.

All your customer cares about is how you're going to solve a problem. That could be making more money, dressing in the most stylish clothes, or losing weight. That's between you and them.

My mission is to get you to forever bury any semblance of marketese on your landing pages.

3. Be Redundant

Anything you say bears repeating. Tell your story when your landing page can accommodate it. Then you know what? Tell the main points again throughout the copy.

You may be sick of it, but the people on your page are hearing it (or reading it) for the first time. You know what that means? They're fascinated by it and you.

In the time it takes them to read your page they won't be tired of it. Trust me. Another thing you need to be excruciatingly redundant about are the benefits. Tell them over and over how great your product is. But, of course, don't lie.

Don't tell them your product can do four loops when it can only do three. Instead, make the three loops the best outcome they could possibly hope for.

4. Never Underestimate Human Greed

We're greedy. YES. I said it. The human race is full of greedy little buggers who want to steal all the gold they can get their hands on. Fortunately or unfortunately we have laws that prevent us from cracking open our neighbors' skulls and stealing his car, or wife, or TV, or anything else we'd like to have.

Lurking deep inside you, me, and every human on this planet is a beast. No matter how much it's fed, the ravenous hunger can never be sated.

Last week, I got an email from Asos. They were holding a sale for 60% off the list price of some brown boots. I didn't need boots. A few weeks before that I'd bought a perfectly adequate pair. I ordered the boots and left the order confirmation page open.

A few minutes later, my partner jumped on my computer and saw that I ordered new boots. She asked me why when I just got a new pair. You know what my reply was?

The deal was too good to pass up. If nothing else, I could give them away at as the perfect gift.

I wonder if the guy I know with seven cars wants another one.

Would the guy I met on a yacht party who has over $15 million pass up on another million? Would people camp out the day before Black Friday to secure the best deals? Do people rush stores on tax free day to save a six measly cents?

Look, I don't know how else to say this. People are GREEDY.

Give them the best bargains, deals, discounts, offers, and service you've ever dreamed of and you'll never worry about "writing good copy."

5.   Never Overestimate Human Intelligence

I consider myself an intelligent man. You may agree since you've read this far into my book. I'm not, by any means, above misunderstanding the most trivial message.

A few months ago I was in the marketplace buying some fresh greens for dinner. My partner calls me up and tells me I forgot something at home (can't remember what at this point). She also called me daddy.

Now, my partner and I have an understanding. Daddy isn't meant for polite company. It's meant for late nights, early mornings, and quickies. I rush home to "pick up what I forgot." I get home, bust through the door, pull off my shirt and she looks at me like I've lost my mind.

Long story short, she sent me back to the market. My confidence was crushed for 12 hours.

Anything that can be misunderstood will be misunderstood. Trust me. Explain it like your prospect is five. If you don't know how then visit the subreddit with the title "explain it like I'm five." Assume nothing. Give details. Lead your prospect by the hand.

Short words. Short sentences. Short paragraphs. Simple English. You can't go wrong. Go back through this book. Have you been forced to open your dictionary once? That's good. I'm communicating.

6. Remember People are Skeptical

I don't trust you. You don't trust me. For all you know, I'm the reincarnation of Jordan Belfort. Instead of stocks, I'm making my fortune with Ebooks.

The number one reason people don't buy is because they don't want what you're selling. I can accept that. It's fair.

The second reason is because they could use the money to do something more important. I'm not and you're probably not selling the cure to HIV so I can accept that as well.

The number three reason is because they don't believe you. They don't believe your product will deliver on its promise. They don't believe they'll ever get it in the mail. They don't believe you're a real business with real people. In short, they don't believe you're honest.

They don't trust you or the ground you walk on. Such is life.

The simple way to get beyond this is to add contact information. Let people shoot an email, pick up a phone, or walk into the office. You have an office right? Or do you work out of your basement? That's ok, let them call, text, or email you.

Reply in a timely manner. Let them know you're around and you care.

7. Get Someone to Critique it

Your mother may not be the best person to ask about the nuances of copy. She CAN help you determine if you've done a good job of conveying a simple message.

Here's what you do.

Ask them to read your copy without any further instructions. Once they're done, ask them what you're selling.

If they can answer clearly then you're on the right path. If they can communicate a benefit or two then you're about to hit a home run. If they tell you they'd like to buy it and pull out their credit card then you've just scored a grand slam.

Privacy policy and TOS
The sad truth is that we live in a litigious society. You've got to let people know what they're getting into.

Put a link to your privacy policy and terms of service where they can see it. It's also a nice touch to let them know their info is safe with you. If you're selling their interest to other businesses then clearly state that in your Privacy Policy and TOS.

Mute the colors so it doesn't create unnecessary anxiety and kill your conversions.

Otherwise, be ready for Sid Vicious, your friendly neighborhood lawyer, to stick something where the sun don't shine.

Social proof that actually matters
When we're in doubt, we follow the crowd. It's called the bandwagon effect and it's a real psychological phenomena.

In low risk situations where we don't know the right socially acceptable behavior, we look to others for guidance. Low risk situations are different depending on the person, but any transaction under $200 is considered low risk. Giving out an email address, downloading something, and starting a free trial also fall into that category.

Think about how you feel about books that don't have any reviews on Amazon. Either no one has bought it because it sucks or it's a new release. Are you ready to take the risk?

Note: Social proof also works in high risk situations, but other factors take precedence.

Not all social proof is made equally. Some suck. The best social proof is specific, backs up your claims, or favorably compares your product to another one.

Testimonials are the most common type of social proof but celebrity endorsements and client logos also work well. Not every testimonial you get will check off all three boxes when it comes to being specific, backing up your claims, and comparing your product to a competitors.

What you'll get are a handful of testimonials that say different things.

One will mention a specific benefit.

Another one will talk about one of your claims.

A different one will compare your product to a competitor. This is good. It shows the variety in your customer base and the utility of your product.

The most powerful testimonials are specific. Instead of saying "I got to my ideal weight faster than I thought possible." A better testimonial would be "I lost 30 pounds in six weeks and I've kept it off for over a year."

Everyone's goals are different so if another person meets their targets, it's not impressive. For all you know, their goal was to lose five pounds. When you show numbers and time, it frames the results that are possible.

When you're copy is already great, the confirmation bias kicks in. This is a psychological phenomenon in which people are more susceptible to information which supports their beliefs. If they've already been convinced by your copy, the testimonials are icing on the cake.

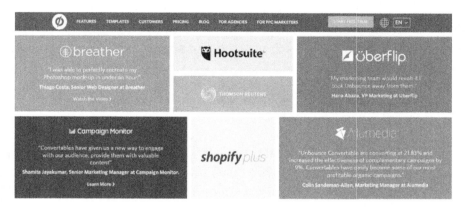

Benefits vs features
A feature is not a benefit and a benefit is not a feature. I see websites try to pass them off as the same thing all the time.

A feature is a fact about your product or service. Your device comes with one terabyte of hard disk space is a feature. You can store all your family photos and videos are benefits. Can you see the difference?

One is subjective and the other is objective.

There's a bit of confusion around this concept. Though it seems straightforward, what you consider a benefit may not be a benefit to the end user. These are called fake benefits.

48

Let's talk about fake benefits for a moment
A fake benefit seems useful or coveted on the surface, but when you place it under scrutiny, you'll see it's not.

"Lose weight naturally!"

What's the benefit there? They want to lose weight like normal people, otherwise, they wouldn't be reading your copy.

"Watch T.V. when you want."

This one also fails to live up to the benefit test. Don't I already watch TV when I want to? If I can't watch T.V. at any given time, your service won't help me.

A better statement would be "watch your favorite T.V. shows on demand." Can you see the subtle difference there?

With one, you claim what you don't have the power to give. You can't affect their schedule. In the second statement, you see the true benefit because you can come home after prime time T.V. is over and still catch the game, or the latest episode of Game of Thrones. You can affect how they access content.

There's a simple test from Clayton Makepeace—a great copywriter—called the forehead slap test. Will your prospect slap themselves on the forehead because your benefit makes so much sense?

"I need to lose weight naturally," or "I need to watch T.V. when I want."

You probably never will and I probably never will.

It'll be an even harder sell for your customers who aren't intimately familiar with your products.

Nobody really wants to lose weight for the sake of losing weight. The real power behind that statement is what can happen if you don't stay in good shape. Public ridicule, lower self-esteem, premature death, predisposition to diabetes which comes with its own host of problems, hypertension, increased risk of stroke, cancer, blindness, kidney disease, heart attack, etc etc.

An overweight person wants to avoid the dangerous complications associated with obesity. That's the real benefit of the fitness program or dieting regime being offered.

Take a step back and take off the lens of the creator. Put on the lens of a user or customer and decide if they'll consider your selling points true benefits.

Features Vs Benefits

Features and benefits can be hard to sort out and easy to confuse — especially when you're close to the message.

Features are facts about what you're offering.

Benefits are the ways it helps them achieve their goals, needs, and desires.

Sure, they know they need to lose weight, make more money, or dress better but they don't know why you're the best person for the job. They may not even know all the reasons and benefits of doing those things.

Ask yourself "and so what?" about every benefit and feature you think you have.

Let's say you're selling phones and one of the features of the phone is 128gb of memory capacity. No matter what your goals or feelings are about the phone, it'll always have 128gb of memory

The phone has 128gb of memory.

And so what?

So you can store more things.

And so what?

Life is less stressful, you don't have to worry about what you download or store because there's enough space to accommodate it. Take as many pictures, record as many videos, and install as many games as you want knowing your phone will always have room for more.

You can do this simple process for anything in any industry.

The awning is double coated with UV repelling paint.

And so what?

Play in the sun all day under our awnings and never think about the harmful effects of the sun's rays on you or your loved ones.

Our shirts or made with patented stain resistant fibers.

And so what?

Your life becomes easier because you won't have to worry about your children messing up their clothes five minutes after being dressed.

Real Benefits Connect Desires
The real benefits to your customers mirrors their desires, wants, and needs. Saving time, cutting costs, making money, becoming healthier, and being happier all qualify.

When you know the real desires of your customers, you can write a string of benefits that touch home every time.

When you don't know the desires of your tribe, your benefits will seem hollow and uninspired.

That's why you've done the research.

That's why you've picked out their exact words.

That's why you took the time to figure out their real objections.

Go through your research and figure out what your customer wants. Not the politically correct answers, but the ones they whisper into their pillows at night. Listen to what they're telling you. At the same time, look at the benefits your competition is offering your customers for choosing them.

Look for ways to structure your message so it taps into their deepest desires. It takes them from where they are now, to where they want to be. Your product is the bridge to get them there.

Perform the "and so what" test on every benefit you list in your subheadings and bullets to make sure it's filling a need/desire.

The offer
The old offer. The do or die section of your landing page. Even if you've crafted the best headline, the perfect copy, and the most powerful testimonials your offer can kill conversions.

The more you want people to give you, the better your offer needs to be.

It's the beginning of your close. When you present the offer, it's time to start pulling out all those copywriting tricks to close the sale.

Whether your offer is free or paid, you're still selling something. It has to be more valuable than what they're giving up (email/money) to get it.

You can present your offer as soon as they land on your page or you can ease into it. As a rule of thumb, paid offers are eased into and free offers are presented up front. This isn't written in stone. Do test it to see which one works best for you.

Let's look at a well presented offer.

In the above image, sage uses an old landing page and converts it to take advantage of Cyber Monday. As you can see, it's short, sweet, and appeals to our greed glands.

They offer two packages and show the savings up front so you know what you stand to gain.

This is one of the bestselling fitness books in the world. The Renegade diet leads with a benefit, *get ripped in 60 days.* Since the promise is for sixty days, they add in a sixty day guarantee. The call to action button stands out on the black background.

The page is much longer than this. They tell you the most important information before presenting the offer for the first time.

Clear Call to action
Never assume. Don't think your prospect knows the next step they're supposed to take. No matter how clear it is to you, it can be like Hebrew to your visitor. The call to action is another opportunity for you to boost conversions. Even though it's not a make or break portion of your page, it can have a significant impact on whether or not your prospect follows through with your desired action.

Craft your call to action with clear language. Leave no room for confusion. When possible, keep it under three words. Examples of calls to action are as follows:

"Get Access to X" Get access to Boss Babes.

"Get your Copy of X" Get your copy of Boss Babes.

"Start my X" Start my Boss Babes Tutorial.

A great way to bring attention to the call to action is to make it a different color from the rest of the page. For example, you can use a red call to action button on a blue page. It'll stand out and draw the eye immediately.

That, coupled with clear language will make sure your audience is able to find and understand the element that'll take them to the next step.

This is the last action your prospect takes before signing up or paying. Sometimes, a simple proceed to checkout is all you need in order to keep them moving. Other times, you'll have to get more creative.

If you've not gotten them already, make sure to download the free worksheets which include the landing page checklist, swipe file, and headline formulas.

https://www.iaexperiment.com/landing-worksheets

Chapter Five: Landing Page Rules

When I was much younger, I had a strong aversion to authority. When you were openly exercising it against me, you could be sure I'd tune you out. That dislike extended to rules. I gleefully broke them every chance I got. I would get the consequences and that'd only reinforce my aversion to authority.

A virtuous cycle—yes?

I'm a rebel. It flows through my veins. It's part of the reason why I'm writing this book and not filling prescriptions in a pharmacy near you.

With that understanding, I hate to call anything a rule. Some things are here today and gone tomorrow with no warning. Rules are broken every day. Some rules fade into the background because we've discovered a better way.

I call this chapter Landing Page Rules with my tongue stuck to my cheek.

I've found a few of the rules to be indispensable because they're based on human psychology. As you know, we're creatures of instinct and intellect. Our intellect evolves much faster than our instinct. For the next thousand years, our instincts will remain unchanged.

Some of the other rules are best practices as of right now. Who knows how the internet will evolve in the next twenty years (by that time, this book will have a fifth edition)?

Just like I told you in the first few pages of this book, test everything. Your business is unique and only you can determine what's best for it.

Now that I've got my monologue about rules out of the way, let's get down to business.

One page one goal
Have you ever tried hardcore multitasking? It starts at 8AM and ends at 4PM. When you look back on your day, you've done almost nothing.

It goes something like this. You've opened ten browser tabs and two of them are your favorite social media sites. You're preparing a report on ad ROI and to top it off, you're listening to the latest Jay Z album.

When you stand up after a long day of work, you've written five hundred words for a blog post and your ROI report is only half done. We won't even touch on the social media posts you were supposed to schedule in Buffer, the calls you planned to make, and the email outreach you told yourself you were going to do.

When a landing page has more than one goal, it's essentially multitasking. It's unable to get its main goal done let alone the fringe assignments you've given it. A landing page with more than one goal might as well be a blog post.

If you want pages to sell for you then make them sell and nothing else.

If you want a page to favorably dispose visitors to your brand then ignore everything else but that goal.

When you want it to collect emails then build the page in a way that emphasizes email signups.

You need to know what you want from the landing page before you write a single line of copy. There are tangible positives to creating pages with only one goal.

1. It reduces the amount of options which ultimately reduces anxiety.
2. You have an easier time writing compelling copy.

Let's look at an example. Let's say you're giving away a PDF with essential lab values for nursing students. In order to download it, they have to give you their contact information. At this point, your prospect doesn't need to know your company story.

To be honest, if you give them too much information right now, there's a real possibility of them getting bored and closing the page.

They don't need to hear about a webinar you're hosting and you can be sure they're not interested in any products. They're on that page for the lab values. Let them know why they need them. Then give it to them.

Only essential imagery
We've spoken at length about imagery in Chapter Four. You're familiar about what kind of images to use and how to use them.

I'm sure you know by now that images increase CTR (click through rates) and your final conversions. Images with attractive people in them may have the highest impact on your visitors. Right behind them are images with women and babies.

Does that mean you should stick a picture of women and children on every landing page you have?

No, of course not.

In fact, I don't have a picture of a baby on any landing page I've ever designed and they're still performing above average. It has nothing to do with the brands I've worked with.

I'm a young man. These women are beautiful. They're also not going to convince me to buy anything. They may get my attention long enough for you to pitch me a product which ties into the image. If it doesn't tie in, I'll just be confused and may feel a bit used.

The problem is that it's easy to go overboard. Maybe you read some research or a case study that said they increased conversion rates by 50% by adding a red image to the page. Does that mean you should test red images at strategic places on your page?

No.

If your image isn't contributing to the written copy in some way then save it for one of your blog posts.

Don't be the person who uses images just to use them. Over time, it'll do more harm than good for your conversions.

Use only real authority
Many business owners walk a thin line. On one side is the truth. On the other side are lies. The line separating the two are where truth and lies merge based on how you present the information.

Foremost in my mind is the way books and authors are presented to an audience. There are dozens of best seller's lists. The most popular are the New York Times, Washington Post, and possibly Amazon. To be a best seller on any of those lists a major accomplishment.

Here's where the grey area starts. Amazon has dozens of categories for their books. Each category has its own best sellers list. Maybe there are three books in a category and an author has the third best-selling. It doesn't matter. She's still a best seller.

Most people wouldn't use it for advertising. Some people will. They'll leave off the fact that they were only competing with three other books. No matter what they did, they'd be a best seller. Their title will look something like, Best Selling Author. It's true but a bit vague.

That's not real authority. It wouldn't be fair to your landing page visitors if you led with that statement. A celebrity using your product or service isn't an automatic endorsement.

It's possible they got your product as a gift from their mother and she forces them to use it. Maybe they bought something, used it, and hated it. Along the way, a picture surfaces and the creator of the product decides to add it to their landing page.

They've taken the name of that authority and abused it. Don't fall into this trap. When in doubt don't do it. When possible, get written endorsements saying they love the product. Never assume.

Whitespace is king

According to Discover Magazine, the eyes and processing apparatus for vision take up about 30% of the brain. More than half of the electrical activity occurring in the brain is dedicated to interpreting visual information.

From the moment you wake up in the morning to the time you go to sleep, your brain is constantly making sense of the world through your eyes. It's a herculean task that doesn't capture most of what we see.

There's just too much going on. We use shortcuts and biases to determine what's important enough to be "seen" and what fades into the background. In a room, the furniture becomes mundane and we react to movement.

Anything that strains the eyes or is difficult to process is promptly ignored. Otherwise, we'd have a breakdown from sensory overload.

Whitespace on your landing pages provides relief for the eye and makes it possible to digest what's been written. Without it, there would be huge blocks of intimidating text.

There are many reasons to use white space. Chief of which is because it makes your text easier on the eyes and more inviting. That's not all.

- Readers easily regain their place when they look away for short periods.
- Breaks the text into sections (headings and subheadings).
- Adds emphasis to certain parts by enclosing them in white space.

In a book, you can get away with denser paragraphs. This is especially true with fiction. In a nonfiction book like this one, the paragraphs tend to be shorter and the sections are broken up with headings. It makes it easier for the reader to get to the parts of the text they find most important. They can skip everything else. That's not possible if your text is one large block from beginning to end.

Online, the need for whitespace is even more apparent. The denizens of the World Wide Web are chronic skimmers. It's what we do to stay sane in an insane world. If you're page isn't easy to skim they won't stick around to read your message and see your offer.

Not everyone on your landing page needs to hear your story (we'll talk more about stage of awareness in Chapter Six). Some people just want to find the benefits and features. How would they do that without subheadings, bullets, and white space?

Don't attempt to give your users everything at once. Concern yourself more with their ability to read and understand what's important over saying everything on your mind.

Tweak load times

A fast website is a higher converting website. Amazon found that 100ms of latency costs them one percent of sales. Over the course of a year, one second slowdown will average out to about $1.6Bn.

Optimizing a website for speed is something that makes me pull my already thinning hair late at night. For every bell and whistle you add, the slower your website becomes. Internet users are an impatient lot.

Four in ten American internet users will abandon a webpage that takes longer than four seconds to load. Mobile browsers only give you three seconds to get your ecommerce page up and running. They could care less about the high definition images you've plastered everywhere so they can see what they're buying. That's your concern, not theirs.

Although speeding up your website is beyond the scope of this book, I'd like to give you a few resources to start your optimization process with.

1. **Google PageSpeed Insights**. They have a few tools for developers to analyze and optimize their websites. They'll give you recommendations about how to improve your load times. If you're not familiar with web development then the recommendations will create more confusion than clarity.

2. **GTmetrix.com**. This is another website to help you increase your website speed. You can analyze individual pages and get a Google and Yspeed score. Their recommendations can be as confusing as Google's. If you're using WordPress, they have a straightforward process you can use to improve the speed of your website.

3. **Pingdom Website Speed Test**. This is another free tool brought to us by Pingdom. It measures your page speed using a server of your choice. When you get the results, it tells you the size of the page, a breakdown of the files, and what's taking the most time to load. They don't, like the other ones, give you speed suggestions.

Each of these websites has accompanying resources to make it easier for you to speed up your website. Unfortunately, speed optimization isn't a one-time deal. Over time, you add more features, get more traffic, and build a repository of content.

Each addition will affect the speed of your website. That translates to constantly working to optimize it.

Keep interest and add value

It's true; the internet has a short attention span. If they're not interested then they're not interested. It'd be easier to use a fire hose to turn off the sun than it'd be to get them to read your page.

On the other hand, it's still possible to lose the attention of someone who's interested. That's the worst outcome. A person lands on your page, is interested in your offer, but bounces because they're bored to death.

Interest is your golden ticket to your prospect completing your desired action. Repeat after me: **I will not write boring copy.**

Boring copy happens when you use jargon no one understands. I like to call it marketese. Boring copy happens when you're talking about yourself more than the needs and wants of your customer. Another way boring copy happens is when you don't know who you're talking to.

These are the most common situations in which boring copy occurs. They are by no means the only situation. Counter boring copy by understanding your audience, writing in a conversational tone (like this book), and highlighting the problem and the transformation.

All of this is well and good, but there's something else you should be doing on your landing pages. It may not be possible for the shorter lead generation pages, but it definitely has a place on your longer sales pages.

Add value.

It's one thing to keep interest. It's another thing entirely to add value. How can you add value on your landing pages?

Let's say you're selling a high quality leather journal for daily writing. A simple way to instantly add value is suggest some of the exercises a customer could do with the journal. You not only give your product more utility, you help them think about what it will be like when they're using it.

Another way to add value would be to teach a bite sized lesson. On a sales page for one of my products, I walk my prospect through a short strategy on Instagram marketing. It's not elaborate, but they can close out the page and implement it instantly and see results.

Add value while keeping attention and you'll see a positive swing in conversions.

Don't exaggerate but still rave
We talked about the thin line business owners walk when we mentioned authority. It's even easier to exaggerate. Here's the thing with exaggerations. No one knows you're exaggerating but you. They either believe everything you say or nothing you say.

The people who eventually complete your desired action believe everything (or most) you say. If you say it'll make them lose 100 pounds in 30 days then you better be sure they get that number or close to it. When they don't, you'll get the angry calls, emails, and refunds that'll show you people pay attention.

You may be able to get away with inflating the number from one million to one million one hundred thousand. Why would you? It's not fair to anyone involved.

Tell it like it is. You're not required to present all your statistics. You're just required to tell the truth when you do present them.

On the other side of the coin is your ability to gush about your products and services. If you can truly help someone lose 100 pounds in thirty days then it's your duty to rave about it. Writing is too subdued these days.

Everyone is worried about offending someone else and using the right politically correct language. I'm not politically correct. I say it how it is as often as I can. If this product is amazing, you better believe you're going to hear about it.

I'm going to make sure you can feel my enthusiasm. My friend, good products are hard to find in this world. There are too many choices between bad and worse. If you've got a good one on your hands, let the world know.

Sit down at your desk, fire up your computer, and RAVE on the page. Let them see your eyes light up, your voice change, and your face flush.

Test everything

The last and most important rule in this chapter is to **TEST EVERYTHING**.

Throughout this book, I've mentioned the importance of using everything I've written as a stepping stone. It's nowhere near the final destination. Much of what works for me won't work for you. Much of what works for you won't work for me.

It's expected.

But it shouldn't stop you from trying and testing strategies until you're sure they're not working or until you've gotten it right. The testing process is more important than the design and creation process.

When you're designing a landing page, you start with a series of assumptions. The tests you perform after the page goes live will either confirm or refute your original guesses.

The simplest and fastest tests to implement are A/B tests. These tests have a control page and an experiment page. On the experiment page, only one element is changed. That could be the button color, the headline copy, the featured image, or anything else you'd like.

Once you have a statistically relevant sample size, you decide which page is the winner and start your next test.

You also have multivariate testing. These ones pit three or more pages against each other at the same time. It takes a significantly larger sample size to determine a winner and may not be viable when you have a smaller budget.

A word about testing. Your goal is to increase conversion rates in a way that'll last. Changing the button color won't help if the offer or the messaging is off. Start with a hypothesis as to why conversion rates aren't where you want them to be and create experiments to test them.

For example, you own a website that focuses on portrait photography. There are different types. You have wedding portraits, family portraits, and graduation portraits. You have separate landing pages set up for each type of portrait.

The landing page for wedding portraits has a significantly lower conversion rate even though you set it up the same way as the other pages.

You create a hypothesis as to what a bride wants when she's looking for a wedding photographer based on your past experience. You then look at whether or not your page clearly communicates those needs. From there, you can make changes and test them against your control page until you've arrived at a long term increase in conversion rates.

Is it something that you'll finish in a day? No.

In Chapter Seven, we're going to focus on a few tools you'll be able to use to make the building and testing process easier.

In the next chapter I want to dive into the how of writing your landing pages. We'll look at how to determine page length, how to know what to include, how to deliver a message that matches the promise, and many other essential writing insights.

In Chapter Eight, we'll spend time with the copywriting formula responsible for billions of dollars in revenue over the years. It's a formula so simple most people overlook it. It's effective and will remain effective for years because it's based on human psychology.

For now, let's look at how to write a compelling landing page.

If you've not gotten them already, make sure to download the free worksheets which include the landing page checklist, swipe file, and headline formulas.

https://www.iaexperiment.com/landing-worksheets

Chapter Six: Writing Hypnotic Landing Pages

Writing the copy for you landing page is the easiest part of the process. It's the last thing you do. Not the first.

It comes after you've done the research, planned the images, and decided who you're talking to. The only task left is fill up the white space with black text.

When you look at like that, it's straightforward. For some reason it's not so easy in practice. I know countless entrepreneurs who have no idea what to say or write on their landing pages. They know what they're selling, they know who they're talking to, and they know what they WANT to say.

The challenge seems to be organizing their thoughts and putting it on paper in a coherent way. That task can be more than a little daunting when you think you have to write a few thousand words. The good news is that you don't.

You don't even have to write up to one thousand words. Hell, depending on the page, you don't even have to write a hundred words. Remember, less is more. Simplicity is king. Unless you're pitching a big ticket item, you'll be perfectly OK with a few hard hitting sentences.

Landing pages are the most focused portions of your website. They're built to convert. Most of your landing pages don't need a long winded explanation. They just need enough information for someone to take your desired action right now.

The level of awareness of your prospect is one of the most important determinants of how long your landing pages need to be. We're going to look at that a little later in this chapter. Other factors you need to take into consideration when writing your landing page are your goals, matching your messages, a clear call to action, formatting, and your tone. We're going to look at each of these major factors in turn and a few minor factors to make sure you write the best landing pages possible.

Start with the end goal

Every successful landing page has a single clear goal. It's the best place to start when you're crafting a high converting page. It informs your decisions about what elements to add and which ones to leave out.

For example, you've got a page for lead generation. Your goal is to get people to download your resource in exchange for an email address. That's it. You don't want that page to do anything else for you.

What do you think you need to write? Would information about how the company started serve any purpose there? Would information about how many customers you have help out? No, it won't.

Every time you add information to your landing page that's not directly tied to your goal, you risk losing the attention of your visitor.

In the above example, the only information they need centers around what they're getting right now. They'll want to know what the resource is (format), how it's going to benefit them, and what they have to give up for it.

You can deliver all that information in a headline and a subheadline.

"Double Your Amazon Ebook Sales with our Ebook: *Amazon Domination*

"Learn the insider secrets to launching successful Amazon Kindle Ebooks on a shoestring budget."

With the above headline and subheadline I've delivered a promise: Double your Kindle sales. It also identifies who can take advantage of the offer: People who don't have much spending cash. I've also been able to tell them the format the resource is going to take: Ebook.

I've done it with twenty four words. Either you want it or you don't. There's no middle ground. When your message is properly matched to what brought them there in the first place then you'll see a great conversion rate.

When you have a paid offer, the goal changes. You want them to pay for something with their hard earned cash. You'll have to go through the process of helping them understand how your product meets their needs and desires.

Just like with the free offer, you provide them with information on what it is, how it helps them, and what they have to give up to get it.

The goal of your page dictates what you write and how long it needs to be.

Everything has only one job

One of my pet peeves is giving aspects of a landing page more than one job. Have you heard those stories about people who've lost organs? The surrounding organs will pick up the load for a while, but in the end, they fail to do the job as well as the original organ.

The same thing happens when you give your headline, subheadline, bullets, headings, and body copy too much work. In their purest form, every word on your page has one primary job; to get your prospect to read the next word.

That's it.

Every word should be meticulously chosen in order to make that happen. As they read one word after another, a narrative will form, they'll become engaged, and perform your desired action. Beyond every word being designed to make the prospect continue reading, the parts of your page have their own duty.

Your headlines job is to keep visitors on the page by reiterating what brought them there in the first place—your promise. The subheadline expands on the benefits in the headline. A hero image is there to enhance the message in the headline and subheadline. Your body copy is meant to warm up your prospect and flesh out the details of your offer. Headings hold interest and allow for easy skimming and comprehension. Bullets are used for eye relief and rapid fire benefits.

Can you see how each part of your page plays a specific role? The addition or subtraction from its job won't be obvious at first. Your prospects won't tell you that your elements are doing too much work. For starters, they don't know and even if they did, they don't care enough to tell you.

The way you'll likely find out is from the dismal performance of your pages. I know that's not the route you want to go. Remember, one element performs one job.

Audience Awareness

These two words will save you a lot of headache and time. Audience awareness is how much your prospect knows about their problem, the solutions available, and your brand. The more aware they are, the easier your job is.

You can spend less time educating them about their problem and more time showing them how you intend to solve it. There are four major levels of audience awareness which we'll discuss in turn.

Each level has different needs and, ideally, different landing pages. Don't worry; once you have the main page set up, it's a straightforward process to create the other pages.

Let's look at the different levels of awareness your prospects will have when they visit your pages.

The Unaware

These are the clueless people wandering around the internet. They land on the pages you create and instead of taking action; they skew your conversion rate. The symptoms of the unaware:

- Don't know about your products.
- Don't know solutions exist.
- Don't truly understand they have a problem.

But there's a silver lining with the unaware. They're the wider market. This is where the bulk of humanity lies at any given moment. That translates into an almost limitless potential for your products and services.

The unaware are the most difficult market to tap because you have to take them through the entire process of understanding their problem, the solutions, and then sell them. Though it has potential, the unaware are difficult to optimize for because they don't know what they want.

They're just as likely to bounce as they are to read the first few paragraphs. The best way to capture their attention is to use stories and educate them without giving away your intention to pitch them.

Long form sales letters (they require the most detailed landing pages) or video sales letters work best in this situation. When creating your landing page, focus on an emotion and or goal. For example, instead of talking about a super duper weight loss supplement, talk about how life will be different after losing fifty pounds.

The probiotics industry uses this technique well.

If you click this ad, you'll be led to a page with a video sales letter. It goes on to tell you about the huge population suffering from a parasite that makes you weak, sick, and other health issues. The way to cure it is to use the probiotic they offer at the end of the sales video.

When you transition into your pitch after telling a story, presenting the problem, and a solution, it'll appear more natural. The more natural it is, the higher your conversion rate will be.

Problem aware

After the unaware, we get to the problem aware. They're a step up from the first group. They understand they're in need of something but have no idea what the solution looks like.

For example, someone knows they need to lose weight but they have no idea there are exercise courses, diet pills, slimming tea, or any other solution. The most powerful way to structure your landing page is to let them know you understand their pain.

You identify with them and you know how important it is for them to solve their problem. In the example of weight loss, you could be targeting middle age women. Identify with their need to look great with their partner, be confident in their skin, and have energy for the kids.

The landing page you craft will be shorter than the first one because you don't need to educate them about the problem. Instead, you reiterate it so they understand they're in the right place. After you establish empathy, proceed to introduce the solution.

When you're a frequent traveler, the 11:00AM checkout time can be a real drag. I've not even started my REM sleep cycle at that point. Art Series Hotels, an Australian brand, launched an innovated solution that addressed a major pain.

It was called Overstay Checkout. Instead of the industry standard 11:00AM check out time, guests were allowed to stay until the new arrivals checked in. They promoted their customer centric message everywhere and were rewarded with increased revenue.

Slack also uses their customer's pain to their advantage.

In the above ad, the Slack team understands we all hate pointless meetings (I dread them with a passion). They use visuals and negative space well to emphasize the pain reducing message. After clicking on the ad, you're taken to a short page that reiterates the promise in the ad and allows you to sign up and test Slack for free.

Solution Aware

Your prospect has moved along from learning about their problem to learning about different solutions available. At the beginning of this process, they don't know your solution exists. When they do find out about you, your job is to convince them your solution is the best one for them.

In the weight loss industry, a prospect knows there are diet pills, exercise courses, slimming tea, and other options available. If they don't choose a solution, you'll also come up on their radar. The job of your landing page is to give them a gentle push.

They know they have a problem and they know there are solutions. The issue now is that they don't know which one will get them the results they need with the least amount of effort.

These pages tend to be shorter and the copy tighter. Prospects are close to purchase and any wrong move on your part will make them bounce.

The best lure for people at this stage are testimonials, case studies, or what sets you apart. A celebrity endorsement also works wonders when you're trying to give someone that final nudge.

Product Aware

Your prospects in this group know about you and the solutions you offer. They're not sure if it's right for them.

Walmart is a popular grocery store. You know you can pick up meat, cheese, and dairy products there. You also know the superstores have a lot of other essentials like lawn care equipment, shirts, and bicycles. The reason you'll experience hesitation about shopping at Walmart is because you don't know if their bikes, shirts, and lawn care equipment are what you're looking for.

The hobby store down the street may have better bikes and also offers killer after sale service. Home Depot may also have a wider range and higher quality lawn care equipment. You also might want to step up a level with your shirt game so you decide to skip Walmart.

Even though your solution solves a specific problem that doesn't guarantee your prospect will take advantage of it. Product aware prospects are looking for specific features in offer. They may want a shirt that's stain resistant. It could be that they need a bike with a special frame because of a medical condition.

Viagra and Cialis are popular drugs. As such, the people visiting their pages should already know what they do. Their copy isn't aimed at educating. Many times, they don't even mention the benefits and what it does. Rather, it's aimed at achieving their desired action—a sale.

The copy you write for these pages is even shorter and tighter than those of the solution aware. Anyone that makes it this far into the research process is ready to buy. Remove the preamble, the stories, all but the most important features and benefits.

These pages ask for the sale quickly and without remorse.

There's another level of awareness called most aware. These prospects have all the information they need to make a decision. They're just looking for the price, the deal, and how to buy it. The pages are short and direct and the conversion rate is always the highest.

Only a small percentage of your prospects will be at this stage of awareness.

Each level of awareness needs its own landing page. If you throw the page meant for the unaware at the product aware then they'll lose patience and leave the page. The same happens if you through a product aware page at the unaware. They don't have enough information to make an informed decision.

At the very least, that's five landing pages for every offer. When you get into different demographics you're showing the offer to, you're looking at dozens of pages.

That would be way to time consuming. Instead, make one master page for the unaware then slice and dice it for each stage of awareness. For example, make a page for a weight loss supplement targeting people in the unaware stage. You'll tell stories, show them the problem, the solution, and testimonials and convince them to buy.

For the problem aware page, cut out the backstory and touch on the problem to show them you understand. The majority of the page will focus on the solution and your offer.

For the solution aware, cut out the problem and the backstory. You only need to mention them briefly. This page will focus on what makes your solution stand out from the competition. Highlight the major benefits and features of the offer and people who've been happy with it in the past. Testimonials and feedback play a major role here.

With the product aware page, they're waiting to pull the trigger. Help them. Highlight your differentiating benefits and features then get out of the way of your prospect.

The page for the most aware is the shortest of all. Think Apple Macbook pages. Here, you're no longer convincing people. Rather, you're telling them how to make the final move.

How do you find out what stage of awareness people are in when visiting your landing pages?

The first indicator of your prospects level of awareness is where they came from. If they land on your page from a link on social media or unbranded search terms, they're likely unaware or problem aware.

Someone that comes from a search engine using branded terms is problem or solution aware. It depends on the key terms they used to search. When your branded keywords are used then they're solution aware. If not, there's a high chance they're problem aware.

Someone that's coming from your email list can be solution aware, product aware, and even most aware. Their stage of awareness depends on how much information you've given them in your email series.

These are rough guides to help you determine the level of awareness of your prospects. Add another layer by asking the right questions on your landing page. Tools like Qeryz and Qualaroo allow you to place unobtrusive popups that ask your users questions.

There are two that have the most impact.

1. How familiar are you with (insert brand name)
    a. Very familiar (been to this site many times)
    b. Familiar
    c. Not very familiar (This is my first time here)
2. What's happening in your life that brought you here today? (text field)

The first question helps you determine the stage of awareness of your visitors. The second questions gives you rich information about how your prospect describers their problem, the referral sources, and optin bait.

You may find out many of your prospects are coming from Facebook which indicates lower end awareness. Once you know that, you could create a lead magnet campaign and drip out educational content about their problem, your solutions, and why you're the best brand for the job.

Note: Only keep these popups on your page for as long as it takes to gather statistically relevant data. Otherwise, you'll be breaking multiple landing page rules.

Message match to USP
Every piece of content you create and offer you put together has a unique selling proposition. It's true whether you did it intentionally or not. A Unique Selling Proposition is a short, clear statement that tells people how you stand out from the crowd and how you're going to add value to their lives.

We can get into a lot of technical jargon about what it is and isn't (I did that in my book *Craft Magnetic Marketing Messages* already) but that's not what this is about. In a nutshell, you tell them what epicness they should expect from you.

You tell them ASAP.

You don't wait until they get ¾ of the way down the page before you let them know there's some awesome thing in store for them.

That's where message matching comes in. Have you ever been on social media and saw a killer benefit driven headline only to be dumped on the homepage? The link you clicked on set up expectations but you were disappointed.

The same thing happens in emails, Facebook ads, PPC ads, and any other place people click on links. When crafting your headlines or messages for these platforms, you need to take where you're sending your visitors into consideration.

Generally, what you promised in your tweet, ad, or email should be reflected in the first few moments after your visitor lands on your page.

Why?

Because if they don't see it, they'll be confused or feel you didn't live up to your promise. Over time, they'll begin to tune you out or unfollow/unsubscribe from communication altogether. When a visitor lands on your page you should:

1. Reiterate what brought them in the first place
2. Let them know what's awesome about your offer.

You don't need to repeat your words verbatim. What you need to do is match the expectations a visitor has when they click on your ad. For example, if I searched for "cheap flights" and clicked on this ad:

I'm told I'll get insider information about how to secure cheap flights. What I'm expecting to see goes like this:

Headline: Flight prices reserved for a certain group of people or cheap flight deals.

USP: A cool way to get those deals for myself, my family, and friends.

This is the page I land on.

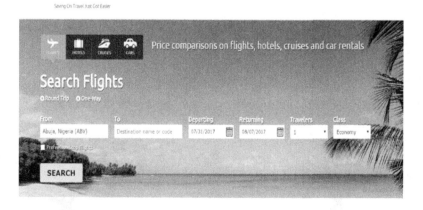

It's the home page. While it's technically a "landing page" it fails to deliver on the promise that brought me to there. It alludes to cheaper prices through comparison shopping. I can think of at least three companies that offer the same thing. It's not something I can't get anywhere else and what I'm seeing doesn't match my expectations.

With message match, the headline and the landing page would be slightly different. Instead of Price comparisons on flights, hotels, cruises, and car rentals, we'd do something more specific. We'd remind and reassure your visitor that they're in the right place.

A headline could go something like this:

Want airlines to compete for your business and get the cheapest flights available?

Search our database to compare the best deals in real time.

Or perhaps:

Do you want the deals airlines will never advertise?

Use our comparison tool to unearth the best deals in real time.

The above headlines and subheadline match the expectations the visitors bring to the page. They're more likely to use the search function and book a ticket if they find what they need.

Your job is to match the expectations your visitors bring to the page. Once they see they're on the right page, you'll still need to hold their attention and get them to take your desired action.

In a nutshell, you're going to state what amazing thing they're going to get at the end of the day.

Not all landing pages work the same. Sometimes, after you match the messages, it may be best to start in on a story. Other times, you'll want to launch right into the highlights of your offer. The only way to find out what works best for you is to test it.

Before you say your landing page doesn't have any unique value, I'm going to cut you off. Every piece of marketing collateral exists to deliver value of some form and move your prospect further to your desired action.

- Why should someone join your weekly newsletter?
- Why should someone buy your products?
- Why should someone trust you to be a service provider?

It's because of the unique value you bring to the table. If you don't know what that is then how will a complete stranger know?

Less is more

I've been harping on about simplicity throughout this book. One thing I learned early on in my teaching career is that things need to be repeated. If you don't repeat it, it may be registered, but no one takes it seriously.

Now, I'm repeating it. Less is more. You don't need those cool gifs, you don't need a dozen images, and you don't need to tell your entire business history.

Reread what you've written and ask yourself, "is this necessary in order for my prospect to understand my message? If I remove it, will my message be compromised?" If the answer is no then cut it without remorse.

If, on the other hand, what you're saying is important, reduce the number of words you use to say it. Most content, unfortunately, is used to fill space. The tighter your copy, the clearer you are and the higher your conversion rates.

Use you – have a conversation
Nobody likes jargon. What we hate even more is feeling like we're being spoken down on. That happens when you're out of touch with the people you're talking to. Even if you're selling to businesses, a single individual will read the page.

She may report to her superior, but that's irrelevant. In order for her to champion your cause you have to convince her. Think of her as a friend you're talking to over coffee. You want to steer this friend in the right direction.

How do you do that?

By coming down to your friend's level. You're an expert in the field, your friend isn't. She's coming to learn from you and seek solid advice. Would you start using industry jargon and talk in the third person? No you wouldn't.

You'd throw all that stuff out the window and get down to the serious business of helping your friend.

Long copy if it's necessary – keep the copy tight
There are no hard and fast rules about whether or not your copy should be long. They say the attention span of people on the internet is lower than ever. I disagree. But you know that already.

Our attention spans are only short when we're not interested. Let's assume you were looking for a book about fitness. No amount of cajoling or psychological triggers will make you stick around and read a page about tires. It just doesn't work that way.

A page with a fitness book or program will grab your attention. You'd want to know everything possible in order to make an informed decision. You also want to know what kind of results you can expect to get.

The first rule of thumb is that the more expensive an item, the more detail someone needs. If you had to buy a car off the internet with only a description and a picture, I'm sure you'd want to know exactly what kind of red it was, the MPG for highway and cities, the horsepower, the type of fuel injection system it used, and a host of other details.

If you're planning on buying a five dollar fidget spinner then you probably just want to know the color and how long it'll take to ship.

You can write long copy. There's nothing wrong with it. Focus on what the customer will find important and remove extraneous details you may think are important. Use the "and so what test "outlined in Chapter Four to ensure you're hitting on the right benefits.

Use bullets points
Bullet points are more or less indispensable on your landing pages. They look good and deliver a lot of information in a short amount of space. They preserve your narrative, add whitespace, and keep people reading.

A bullet point is equivalent to a breath of fresh air. In the digital world, everything revolves around brevity and attention. The bullet point bridges the gap between length and utility. Bullets should:

- Express a clear benefit or promise – think of them as headlines
- Be as close to the same length as possible (including number of lines)
- Keep a similar theme. EG begin with same part of speech or grammatical form
- Keep in mind that they're not always sentences (stick with paragraphs for that).

Those are a few general guidelines when writing your bullet points. The draw of bullets is their ability to break down larger pieces or lists into a digestible format.

They make your content more comprehensive. If your page isn't understood then it's all for naught.

Bullets can be used to draw a user into your copy, keep them reading your copy, or trigger a purchase. Let's look at the actual writing process so you can give your conversions a much needed boost.

You're going to be using curiosity to make the most out of your bullets. Curiosity isn't an adequate word. You're going create curiosity so strong that it evolves into an engrossing need on the part of your prospect. They have to know what's next or how to get the benefits you outline in your bullets.

A few examples of engrossing bullets:

- How to detect and protect yourself against a parasite that kills thousands of people every year.
- The simple yet overlooked strategies to double your sales without any extra traffic.
- How to drink alcohol without ever getting a hangover

Once you understand the curiosity gap, it's simple to write engrossing bullets. Take any group of benefits you have and write it in such a way that'll spark curiosity.

Let's say your benefit is the ability to lose thirty pounds in thirty days. That's cool but also bland. Instead, let them know they don't have to do something hard that's expected. That bullet point will transform into How to lose thirty pounds in thirty days without killing yourself in the gym.

We just got a curiosity evoking bullet without much effort. Let's try it again.

Let's say your benefit is insider knowledge about two medicines that, when used together, can cause ulcers. How will you write that to engros your reader?

Learn two common cold medicines which you've likely used that, taken together, skyrocket your chances of developing an ulcer.

Try it with your benefits and you'll see your conversions rise (the headline formulas in the worksheets also work well when crafting engrossing bullets).

Keep paragraphs short
I've been using short paragraphs. I've also been using short sentences. It's from my experience with blogging and writing on the internet. I can't help it. Before I know it, I'm hitting the "." key and right after that, I'm hitting the "enter" key.

No one wants to read huge blocks of text. They don't want to do it on the internet and they don't want to do it in a book.

This isn't just a good habit I picked up after years of writing. There are tangible reasons why you should always keep your paragraphs to three to four sentences.

1. The users of the internet scan until you give them a reason not to. They read the beginning, and end of each paragraph to find interesting information. When your text is in one big block it makes it impossible to scan.
2. Short paragraphs make for easy reading. Large blocks of text are intimidating. It scares you and I on a subconscious level. In addition to that, it's difficult to hold your place when you look away for a moment.
3. Easier to get down the page. The most important thing when someone lands on your page is for them to keep reading. The shorter your paragraphs, the faster they get down your page. When they come up for air, they're already a quarter through with it.
4. Easier to avoid mistakes. It's almost too easy to make a mistake with compound complex sentences. Short sentences and paragraphs highlight and reduce your writing mistakes.
5. White space. I dedicated an entire section to this. Short paragraphs add the all-important white space to your writing

which is easy on the eyes and gives the illusion of brevity. No matter how long it truly is.

Short paragraphs are powerful. Long sentences also have their place. Don't think you need to make every paragraph you ever write four sentences or less. Only the ones on your landing page are forced to adhere to this rule.

F-type Landing page design
We don't look at landing pages the same way we look at pages in a book. When you're reading a novel, you'll look from the left to the right. That's the way the English language is set up.

The way we view landing pages is quite different. We start at the top right then move over to the top left. We then go down the page a bit and glance over to the right. From the right, we swing back over to the bottom left.

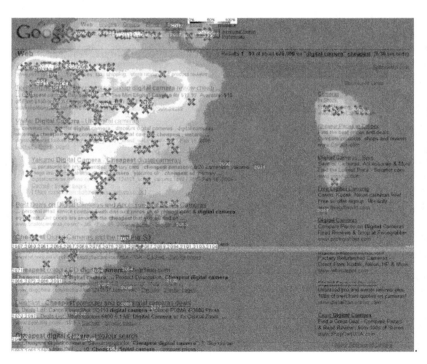

After we've taken everything in, we'll start over at the place that caught our attention the most. You can design yours to take advantage of that.

Put your most important elements like a headline or image on the top right hand side of the page. The next most important element goes to the left of it on the same level. Right below that, continue your copy or any other elements you want your prospect to view.

Everything you see here is above the fold on the AdEspresso landing page. They have an image that promotes trust, a succinct value proposition, and graphic illustrations of the features within the membership.

Let your customers write it for you
The best landing pages don't use your words.

They use the words of your customers. Every time they email you, call you, or leave a review they're saying something about your products and services. I have a folder on my desktop full of the thoughts and words of my customers.

90

All you have to do is listen and half of your landing page is written for you. When you want to write a headline, create an A/B split test with your ideas and the words of your customers.

When you're thinking about what to use as benefits use the things your customers have pointed out to you. Why do they buy? Why do they sign up? Why do they read what you've written?

If you don't have any customers or don't have feedback, go to the forums you know they hang out in. Every industry has a few high traffic forums you can look at.

Open Google Chrome or navigate to google.com. Once there, type in "niche + forum" without the quotation marks. Google will bring back more results than you can ever look through.

> **Fitness Forum | Gym in London ON | Canada's Top Fitness Club**
> fitnessforum.ca/
> At Fitness Forum in London, ON, our gym memberships include fitness classes, and access to our gym amenities including swimming pool & squash courts.
>
> **Fitness Forum Fitness Centre Member Services | Gym in London, ON**
> fitnessforum.ca/services/
> Fitness Forum provides all the services you need to transform your body Click any of the links below to read more about a particular service or just scroll.
>
> **Nerd Fitness Rebellion: Forums**
> https://rebellion.nerdfitness.com/
> Forums .... NerdFitness Suggestions. Have ideas or suggestions on how I can improve Nerd Fitness? Have a suggestion for an article? Post them here!
>
> **Health and Fitness Forum - Two Plus Two Forum**
> forumserver.twoplustwo.com › Other Topics
> Health and Fitness - Discussion of health and fitness.
>
> **best fitness forum - Scooby's Workshop**

Select a few of the promising ones and click through to the website. Look at the most popular threads that are in line with your business. Those could be questions people commonly have, insights, case studies, or whatever.

⊞ 2016 Triple Bypass or bust, a bicycle log (🗎 1 2 3 4 5 6 7 8 9 ... Last Page) unfrgvn	Today 12:02 PM by Marn	335	22,507
⊞ Josie 2.0 (🗎 1 2 3 4 5 6 7 8 9 ... Last Page) Very Josie	Today 11:51 AM by Very Josie	1,074	26,065
⊞ Montecore tips his fedora at Snitch/3/1 (🗎 1 2 3 4 5 6 7 8 9 ... Last Page) Montecore	Today 11:46 AM by Montecore	6,008	225,473
⊞ Training for a 300km/186mile bike ride (🗎 1 2 3 4 5 6 7 8 9 ... Last Page) Marn	Today 11:21 AM by unfrgvn	272	12,480
⊞ Thremp - No More Fatties - The Return (🗎 1 2 3 4 5 6 7 8 9 ... Last Page) Thremp	Today 10:55 AM by Malucci	2,048	155,310
⊞ Malucci is a FPOS! (🗎 1 2 3 4 5 6 7 8 9 ... Last Page) Malucci	Today 10:25 AM by Malucci	2,582	168,183
⊞ 2K Row for a CrossFit WOD mxp2004	Today 10:16 AM by mxp2004	6	106
⊞ Beeschnuts Strength Training Log (🗎 1 2 3 4) beeschnuts	Today 10:04 AM by beeschnuts	98	2,877

What you're looking for here is the language your customer uses to describe their problem and how they describe the ideal solution to it. Look for patterns and terms specific to your industry.

Forums aren't the only place you can look for what customers in your industry are saying. You can repeat the process with Facebook groups, Reddit, Quora, and any other high trafficked site with a lot of user generated content.

Chapter Seven: Choosing the Right Software

They say software is eating the world. I'd have to agree. Right now, there's software for almost anything you can imagine. I've been hooked on a mobile app for the past two weeks.

You know what it does? It keeps my schedule. It's a calendar. It's all black, sexy, and easy to use.

Is it the first, the last, or the best calendar app to hit the market? No on all fronts. Why do I love it so much then? To be honest, I don't know. I think it has something to do with how slick it looks. Apart from that, it meets my needs and allows me to be better organized.

The same is true for landing page software. There are a lot of options out there and if you're not careful, you'll be switching around. When you switch, the old pages have to be exported (if you're lucky) and uploaded to the new software.

That's the best case scenario. A problem I've run into with the wrong software is its inability scale with you. I remember one of the first landing page software I bought didn't allow me to A/B test.

At the time, it didn't matter much to me. I was just trying to send traffic to a page and hope it'd convert. I used that software for a long time. Before I knew it, I had dozens of pages.

Once I became more sophisticated, I wanted to do things like add HTML tracking code, A/B test, create timed offers and so on. I got a rude awakening when I tried to use the software I had. It contained a fraction of the features I wanted.

Even the features they did have were poorly implemented and were more of a liability than a benefit. I'd like to save you from that fate. I'm going to introduce you to four landing page software suites I've used in the past.

Hopefully, you'll find what you're looking for. If not, let me give you a few criteria when you strike out on your own.

1. **The traffic should always be unlimited**. You don't know how long and how quickly you're going to grow your business. For now, a cap of 10,000 visitors a month may seem like more than enough. What about three years from now. That traffic may only be a drop in the bucket. When it happens, you have two options. Pay an exorbitant amount for an unlimited traffic plan or move over to a different service. Neither option is ideal.

2. **Easy integration with tools you already use**. You're already using a few tools to get the most out of your time and energy. At the very least, you have email marketing software, analytics software, and a payment processor. Will your landing page

provider integrate with the one you're using now and other ones you may use in the future?

3. **It needs to be able to track all your most important metrics**. We spoke about the most important metrics of landing pages in Chapter Two. Does it track that information accurately?

4. **An intuitive interface is a must**. There are too many pieces of software out there. In order to get up and running quickly, their user interface needs to be easy to learn. Preferably a drag and drop builder that lets you add HTLM or CSS at will. Otherwise, you'll only be able to use a small portion of the power inherent in most of these tools.

Use the above criteria as a guideline. Add any other criteria you find important to your situation. I've used a lot of landing page software over the years so it'll be difficult for me to talk about all of them. I'll give you a short review of four of my favorite. If you like any of them then check them out and sign up.

If not, start your search and see where it leads you.

Lead Pages

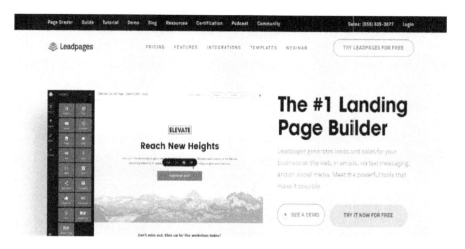

Leadpages is one of the most popular landing page software providers available on the internet. As of this writing, they have over 45,000 customers. They're most popular in the internet marketing niche, but are used in every industry.

The software easily integrates with your website so you'll be able to add them to your main domain as pages. Or, if you want them to host the page for you, it's simple to set up a subdomain with a CNAME redirect. The main draw of the second option is increased speed.

Leadpages comes packed with a lot of features which I'll get into in a moment. One of the problems you may experience when using he software is a steep learning curve. They do have a responsive support team and a dedicated group of developers which can help you out if you experience any issues.

Leadpages has one of the largest libraries of pre designed templates for you to use. They come with over 140 to be used as is and another 80 or so which can be customized with a drag and drop editor. The templates are not interchangeable. The predesigned ones cannot be used with the drag and drop editor.

One of the most powerful features of the templates is their ranked conversion rates. Leadpages has been tracking the numbers on their templates across different industries for years. You can choose the one with the highest conversion rate right out the gate and customize it with your text.

They also have a marketplace where you can buy pages ranging from seven to thirty nine dollars. Of all the templates they offer, my favorite ones are the upsell pages and thank you pages which you can use to offset your advertising costs (we'll talk more about that in chapter nine).

In addition to templates, you can build your pages from scratch using their drag and drop editor. Before I continue, I have to let you know that there are two editors. One is the standard editor which has limited functionality. The other is more recent and it has more flexibility.

The software also lets you A/B test your pages against a control. It's available for everyone on a pro plan or higher. If you select the lowest tier, you won't be able to take advantage of it. Keep that in mind because Leadpages has premium pricing. It's one of the more expensive solutions on the market.

An interesting feature is Leaddigits. Customers can optin to your mailing list by texting a phrase to a five digit phone number. They'll get a text back asking for their email. It's a nice touch to get leads in person at a conference or other event.

The analytics is clean and gives you the most important information. You see visitors, unique visitors, and conversion rates.

Another powerful feature of Leadpages is Leadlinks. You paste them into a broadcast email through your email marketing service. When your subscribers click the link, they're automatically added to the list connected to the landing page you send them to.

For example, you're promoting a webinar. When your subscriber clicks the link to join the webinar, they don't have to fill out a form. They're automatically added to the list. It's a seamless process that reduces drop-offs from your landing pages. Leadlinks is only available on pro packages and up.

Over half of all internet traffic has gone mobile and Leadpages took that into consideration. All of your pages are automatically rendered so they'll be mobile friendly.

One of the most popular features and to some, the most important, are Leadboxes. These are two step optins you can insert directly into a post. They don't activate until someone clicks on a link in your post. Once they do, a targeted optin or content upgrade will appear. These have some of the highest conversion rates for lead generation.

Unbounce

Unbounce was founded in 2009 and has been helping entrepreneurs and marketers build landing pages ever since. They've amassed over 10,000 customers. In addition to providing amazing software for their customers, they create courses, webinars, and Ebooks that'll help you take your landing page optimization to the next level.

As of this writing, Unbounce is one of the only landing page software solutions with a free plan. The next pricing tier they offer starts at $49 a month.

The Unbounce feature set is wide and varied. Like other landing page builders, you can choose a theme to start with. You have the option of just changing the text or adding and removing elements. Unlike Leadpages, you also have the ability to customize everything.

Although you don't need coding skills to use Unbounce, you will have to dedicate some time to learning it. They give you a lot of power to customize your pages. With that power comes a learning curve. You won't be able to create and publish a complicated page from scratch. If you're in a hurry, it'll be a good idea to use one of the templates.

Once you get the hang of it, you'll be able to create and publish landing pages within a few minutes. Using the editor, you can add lightboxes, buttons, forms, timers, and a host of other elements to create the page you need. You can download them to reuse as a custom template or save to your backend.

If you need more power than the elements in the editor offer, you can use custom HTML, CSS, and JavaScript to get your desired effect.

The team at Unbounce took mobile usage into consideration. All of their pages are mobile optimized and you can view your pages with different screen sizes to make sure they're properly optimized.

They integrate with the major email marketing services. Most of the large players like Mailchimp, Aweber, and Getresponse integrate seamlessly. They don't stop there, you can also integrate with webinar software and other third party apps such as Zapier to get the results you need.

One area Unbounce is lacking is its ability to integrate directly with your website. A huge portion of the internet runs on WordPress. All of my websites run on WordPress and there's no way for you to integrate directly with it through plugins from Unbounce. In addition to that, you can't publish your pages directly to Facebook. Take this information into consideration before choosing this app.

They take A/B testing seriously and make it easy to tweak your pages. Just click on the variant button on the top left and it'll duplicate your current page. From there, systematically test different elements until you've gotten the best possible conversion rate on your page.

With a powerful tool like this, you're bound to run into some issues. They have a robust knowledge base and the support team answers in a timely manner. They offer three options for support: email, live chat, and telephone calls. They have specific hours of operation so if you discover a problem at midnight you'll be out of luck.

In the end, Unbounce is an amazing tool to get landing pages up and running in a timely manner. It's not perfect, but no software is. The few issues they have are easily surmountable if you're willing to learn. The biggest deal breaker may be the inability to integrate directly with your website. If you can overlook that then you're in good hands.

Instapages

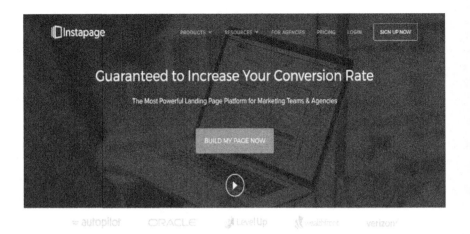

I've used Instapages on and off for over a year. They have one of the easiest interfaces of all the software I've used. Their drag and drop editor is easy to understand and only takes a few minutes to learn.

A feature that threw me off with Instapage was the inability to A/B test your landing pages on their lowest plan. Testing is such an important feature of landing page design and optimization that I was initially put off about trying the product.

When I did sign up, it was through a six month deal and I loved what they'd created. In order to use it properly, I suggest you go with the second tier or higher. Otherwise, the lack of A/B testing severely limits your ability to make irresistible landing pages.

Let's look at some of the most valuable features Instapge has.

One of the first things I look for when choosing a piece of software is its ability to integrate with other software. I have a low touch business model and need my software to work together. Instapage does this by integrating with over a dozen email marketing services.

In addition to email marketing services, you can publish your pages directly to Facebook or integrate with your WordPress site.

I use ActiveCampaign and it's well represented with most software that provides third party integrations. When creating a new page with Instapage there are multiple options to choose from.

- Import from URL
- Drag and drop builder
- Upload a .instapage file

My gripe with this is that you can't upload or download an HTML of your file. Make sure you take this into consideration before you sign up with them. Unless you find a workaround, all the files you download from Instapage are in their proprietary file format.

Instapage has over a hundred templates to choose from. You never have to start from scratch if you don't want to. They don't track customer usage data so I can't say how effective the templates are. At the very least, they look great.

The templates are divided into different categories such as lead generation, click through, or webinar registration. It makes it much easier to find what you're looking for and start building your page.

The design interface is one of the easiest I've used. Their buttons are labeled with clear language which cuts down on your learning curve. I can't tell you how many times a tool tried to be cute by making a branded name for a feature and ended up confusing me.

A few of the menu options are Fonts, Conversion goals (important because some pages need a sign up while others need a click through), Analytics (add your Google tracking code here), SEO, and HTML/CSS.

The reporting features are straightforward and let you keep track of total traffic to a page and conversions. You can even determine how much traffic goes to a split test variation. This could come in handy when you just launched a new variation and want to test it against a control. The control already has a proven conversion rate so you want to catch up to make a statistically relevant decision. You can send 80% of the traffic to the new variation and the remaining traffic goes to the control.

The support is tiered based on your plan. The basic plan comes with email support while the higher levels come with chat and call support. I did have an issue with a few pages I built with the tool overriding my existing pages. It took over a week for them to build out a patch.

Another problem was the inability to add HTML forms. If your email marketing software isn't on their list of integrations, there's no way for you to integrate manually.

Overall, it's a unique tool that's been able to balance ease of use with customization power. If you can afford the second tier plan or above then I say go for it.

Instabuilder 2.0

When you land on the Instabuilder 2.0 homepage, it can be off-putting. The way it was designed makes you think it's one of those internet scams. I wish the people behind it would update the page.

That notwithstanding, it's a robust tool that packs many of the features you'd expect from landing page software without the monthly subscription. That's a good thing and a bad thing. It's good because you get a lot of power with a one off payment. It's a bad thing because they don't release updates nearly as often as the other options in this chapter.

Apart from that, Instabuilder 2.0 is a powerful tool, especially for long form sales pages.

First, they've got templates. I know I've mentioned this with all the other pieces of software in this chapter. That's because I consider it important. It's not easy to build pages from scratch every single time. There are those moments when you need something and you need it now.

They're categorized into many areas such as squeeze pages and sales pages. Whenever you create your own page, you have the option of saving it as a template or exporting it as an html file to be uploaded wherever you like.

Moving on from the templates, there are a lot of customization options baked into the product. You have control over everything from the background color to the metadata.

The process for adding forms, arranging elements, and customizing text is simple. To the left of the screen, you add your element and to the right of the screen, after clicking on the element, you customize it. Once you play with the tool for a while you'll be right at home.

Though it's a drag and drop editor, you can't place elements wherever you'd like. The designers of Instabuilder 2.0 decided to use a grid function. You place elements on the page and they snap into the closest available place.

It can take a bit of getting used to. Once you do, you'll be able to predict how your pages will turn out and what you can and can't do with the tool.

They integrate with other software such as Facebook and GoToWebinar. This gives you the ability to capture leads for your webinar pages and publish directly to your Facebook page. They also allow you to run A/B tests with the click of a button and decide how much traffic goes to each variation.

The analytics leave a bit to be desired. They'll tell you your total visitors but the conversion rate calculations are a bit skewed. I ran a promotion with Instabuilder 2.0 and got 300 email subscribers. According to the software, I only had two conversions. If I didn't know what I was doing, I'd think the fault was from me.

They don't integrate directly with many email marketing services, but they do allow you to add the HTML code of the forms. Because of that, it has more flexibility than some the tools I've mentioned in this chapter.

The major gripe I have with this software is the support team. They don't seem to be native English speakers and instead of tackling your problem individually, they'll refer you to a lot of knowledge base articles. Though they may get the same question pretty often, it goes a long way to address customer concerns on a personal basis.

Instabuilder 2.0 is a robust tool that gives you a lot of customization options but leaves a lot to be desired when it comes to accurate analytics. Data is life. Use this tool if cash is tight and you can only afford a one off payment.

Of the four landing page tools I've presented in this chapter I do have a favorite. Instapage is my tool of choice. It strikes a great balance between customization and ease of use. Most tools stray too far to one side or the other. It's also competitively priced so almost anyone can afford it.

In addition to the features and benefits, they're constantly asking for and delivering improvements to the app. The customer support is top notch and knowledgeable.

I've said it before and I'll say it again. Use what works best for you. If not, you'll curse me in your waking hours and dream about my downfall. No one wants that, especially me.

In the next chapter, I'm going to take you through an old copywriting technique that's responsible for billions of dollars in revenue. It's simple but effective and will never go out of style.

Wondering why?

Read the next chapter.

Before you do, make sure you get the worksheets that come with a checklist, swipe file, and headline formulas.
https://www.iaexperiment.com/landing-worksheets

Chapter Eight: The AIDA Formula

Since the beginning of time, men have tried to convince each other to take their desired action. Sometimes they used force. Other times they used a common goal. Still other times, they appealed to their emotions. Human interaction is nothing but a series of persuasive acts. Either you're being persuaded or doing the persuasion.

Thousands of years ago Aristotle formalized the process of persuasion and called it Rhetoric. It has three parts:

1. **Ethos.** This deals with the speaker and their ability to appear credible to their audience. To pull this off effectively, you need to have competence, good intentions, and empathy. The factors

that affect the perception of ethos in the context of a landing page are word choice, design, formatting, and imagery.

2. **Pathos.** This deals with the emotional influence you have on your audience. No matter the emotional state in which they arrive, you systematically move them to where you want them to be. At that state, they're more susceptible to your message. In order to write effective copy, you need to understand which words, phrases, and devices elicit emotional responses in your audience and use them accordingly.

3. **Logos.** This is the final appeal to logical reason. We use facts to tell and emotions to sell. Both are important. Without the facts, people won't be able to justify their purchase afterwards. If they can't justify it then they'll have buyer's remorse. With buyer's remorse your returns will be high. To make logos effective, different forms of proof are needed. On your landing pages, this comes in the form of testimonials, social proof, guarantees, etc.

We knew this a thousand years ago, but we were limited in our reach.

During the early stages, only the people you could talk to face to face could hear your message. Afterwards, you could communicate with people in a stadium. Move a few years into the future and it was possible to write your words on paper and distribute it throughout your community.

Now, in the information age, there's no limit to how far and fast your message can spread. Even though the medium has changed and the speed is almost instant, one thing remains constant – human psychology.

A few decades ago, a few smart individuals discovered that we go through the same basic steps before we take action on anything. That could be going to war, having sex, or buying something. They built on the teaching of Aristotle and created what's known as AIDA.

The first step is to grab attention. Without attention you can't do anything. After you have their attention, your job is to pique their interest. When you have their interest, you're next task is to inflame their desire. Finally, you **get them to take action.**

AIDA is an acronym for attention, interest, desire, and action. In this chapter, I'm going to break down how to use one of the most powerful copywriting techniques available.

Before we jump in, it's important to note that the formula only works as hard as you do.

What do I mean by that? I mean you need to understand your prospects and customers. You have to know what they want and what they could care less about. There is no shortcut here (for more information on how to do market research, check out my book *Craft Magnetic Marketing Messages* in the Amazon store).

Attention
Attention starts with a compelling headline. We've spoken at length about headlines. Refer back to Chapter Four for a refresher. A headline isn't the only way to grab your reader's attention. You can also use an image that relates to them and your product or a video.

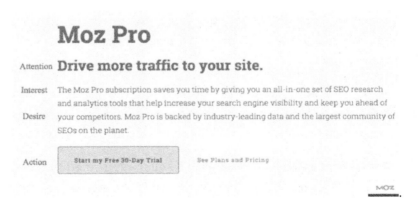

When crafting your headline, ask yourself a few simple questions.

- What's the problem you're solving?
- What's the major benefit of solving that problem?
- What language do they use to talk about their problem?
- Can you make the solution specific to them?

When you know the answers to the above questions you're able to create headlines that speak to them. For example, you give dancing classes for couples and you know people aren't interested in dancing as much as they're interested in strengthening their relationship.

You also know that dancing is a strong relationship building tool. Many of your customers have told you how much closer they feel to their partner after learning to dance with them.

A headline you craft wouldn't lead with your wonderful dance offer. They don't care about dancing. Instead, your headline would lead with strengthening their relationship.

"Do you want to know a surprisingly simple way to build a stronger relationship?"

"These couples have taken their relationships to the next level by doing something no shrink will ever recommend–and you can too."

In both of these headlines, we've led with the end benefit of taking dance lessons. The only reason you've been able to do that is because you know the benefits of your product or service, who your customer is, and what they desire.

Another example could be a weight loss product. You know your customers are women between the ages of thirty five and fifty five. They're married and have a few children living with them. They don't want to lose weight only because it'll make them healthier. They want to lose weight for tons of reasons. Health may be much lower on the list of their true desires.

They want to lose weight so they'll be attractive to their partner. They want to lose weight so they can keep up with the kids. Or they want to feel vibrant and creative. There are so many reasons besides the obvious health concerns.

"Is it getting harder and harder to keep up with your growing family?"

"Become more vibrant and creative with a few simple tweaks."

It's important to use headlines that pull as opposed to headlines that push. An example of a headline that pushes could be "I've got just the thing you've been looking for and its….." How do you know what I've been looking for? Sorry, I'm not interested.

Interest

Attention is the first step. It may be the most important step but that doesn't mean the other aspects should be done in a haphazard manner. Interest follows right on the heels of your attention grab. After you get them to click through to your page, you start to build interest immediately.

People scan webpages. Unless you give them a reason to read it then that's exactly what they'll do. In his book *Advertising Secrets of the Written Word* (recommended read) Joe Sugarman called this process falling down the slippery slope.

Your headline was to get them to the precipice of the slope and the next few paragraphs are the fall. When your headline is compelling, you need to follow up immediately or your prospect will lose interest in what you've got to say.

Remember I said the job of a word is to get you to read the next one? You get them to keep reading by providing interesting information that creates more than a little interest.

Use facts or tell a story. The route you take depends on the product you're selling and what you're asking for. You can go easier on the interest when you're only asking for an email address. If you're selling a two thousand dollar computer then you may have a bit more work ahead of you.

iMac   Design   Performance   OS X   Built-in Apps   Tech Specs

iMac

<small>Attention</small> Retina. Now in colossal and ginormous.

<small>Interest</small> The idea behind iMac has never wavered: to craft the ultimate desktop experience. The best display, paired with high-performance processors, graphics and storage — all within an incredibly thin, seamless enclosure. And that commitment continues with the all-new 21.5-inch iMac with Retina 4K display.

<small>Desire</small> Like the revolutionary 27-inch 5K model, it delivers such spectacular image quality that everything else around you seems to disappear. Adding up to the most immersive iMac experience yet — and another big, beautiful step forward.

Using our dancing example, what do you think you can use to pique the interest of your prospect?

For starters, you can tell the story of past students. How dance lessons helped them learn more about themselves and each other. They became the life of parties and all eyes were on them when they jumped on the dance floor. You can finish up by telling your prospect about how the couple later went on to compete and win in local as well as national competitions.

The aspects you highlight when you build interest will be a reflection of what matters to your visitor. As a dance instructor, you won't talk about how people get in better shape because that's not what they care about.

For the weight loss example talk we could tell a story of a woman who lost thirty pounds and had more creative energy. Or we could touch on how another woman was able to participate more in the lives of the kids. Instead of being a sideline mom, she was the first person they called on because she had so much energy.

Notice how we're approaching the problem indirectly with our stories. We're illustrating the benefits without saying what we're solving outright. For sensitive issues like relationship troubles or self-image, it's better to allude to it rather than stating a problem outright.

Other problems like athletes foot, certain disease conditions, home repairs, etc can be spoken about openly.

As a rule of thumb, when writing long copy, your first three hundred words need to be riveting. It's part of the reason books have introductions and forewords. They're meant to hook you and give you a reason to keep on reading.

Desire
Once you've established interest, you run smack dab into desire. They're different beasts. I may be interested in a pretty girl as a human being but I feel no desire in my loins. The same holds true for your prospect.

They may be interested in what you're saying, but they have no desire to make it part of their lives. In short, they don't want to buy what you're selling no matter how cheap it is. There are three major ways to elicit desire in your copy:

- Go hard with the benefits
- Show or explain how your products can solve their problems
- Paint a picture of the transformation they'll have
- Include testimonials from other customers.

This part is important because a shift takes place in their minds. Your offer is no longer abstract; it's something that can change their lives. It's no longer a piece of marketing collateral for your company. Now, it's something they can use to get results for themselves.

This is where ownership begins.

With the example of dancing lessons for the couple, we've already used stories to paint a picture and pique interest. It's time to hammer on the benefits. Your bullet points will come in handy here. Succinctly list out the relevant benefits to their relationship and other benefits.

That could read something like this:

- Stronger psychological connection.
- Better understanding of your partner's physical abilities
- A way to bring life to any social gathering
- Pick up a new hobby that'll serve them for years
- The perfect date night activity

I'm not a dance instructor so I'm sure I'm missing a few benefits. That's why your research is so important. You need to know what your prospects think they want and what they truly want in the context of your solution.

In the weight loss example, you can show before and after pictures that highlight a striking change. You can use video testimonials in which people give details of how their life was transformed. Don't forget the myriad benefits you're offering your prospects with your solution.

Emotions play an important role in the desire portion of AIDA. If you can't elicit the right emotions in your visitor then they'll never take action. Use words you know bring out the right feelings in you then tweak and test until you have a winner.

After you've successfully brought out the desire in your prospect, the only thing left is to get them to take action.

Action

You've done a good job to get your prospect this far into your landing page. You deserve a pat on the back. The last part is often the hardest. They've read this far because they're interested. You know that. The only problem is that they have a few objections.

There will always be objections.

I remember I was traveling through Nigeria. I have a lot of family there. When visiting someone, it's proper to bring a small gift from your journey. It doesn't need to be anything fancy. You can get away with bread and fruits.

I was in the capital city, Abuja, visiting one of my aunts. As I walked through the door and presented my gift of bread and bananas she took them without a second thought and welcomed me into her home. We chatted and caught up for hours.

The next morning, as is customary, I expected to see the bread on the table as part of our breakfast. The bananas were there but there was no bread. After the meal, I asked her why she didn't bring it out.

She told me it had bromate. I was confused. She explained that they used bromate in some of the bread to make it rise faster. It wasn't good for the body, especially the kids. I felt like a fool. She didn't think anything of it.

That was her insurmountable objection. No matter what I would've said, she wouldn't have changed her mind.

Your visitors also have objections. Some of them will be deal breakers and some of them won't. Your job is to understand them and tackle them head on before you present the desired action.

Common objections include qualifications, satisfaction, money back guarantees, etc.

In the example of the dance lessons, the qualifications of your instructors may be a sticking point. Let them know where they were trained and their experience. You can also introduce scarcity into the equation by limiting the available slots every week.

What about satisfaction? Give them a money back guarantee. If they don't feel their lesson was worth what they paid then you'll refund them the full purchase price. When you give a guarantee, there's a deeper level of trust. You must stand by your product if you're confident enough to refund their money based on subjective criteria.

The action section is also a great place to introduce any bonuses you might have been hiding up your sleeve. Always remember to add a clear call to action. Your visitor can't read your mind and they won't try to.

Unless they're highly motivated, they won't stress themselves to figure out what the next action should be. That's your job.

As you can see, AIDA is a straightforward concept and with a bit of practice, you'll have it down pact. I want to show you an old ad to illustrate the power of these elements in action. I'll also recommend a copywriting resource that's as funny as it is invaluable.

Times Orange County Classified Ads

A DYNAMIC SECTION OF THE WEST'S LARGEST SELLING NEWSPAPER/1375 SUNFLOWER, COSTA MESA/CIRCULATION: DAILY 188,406/SUNDAY 221,142

To place your ad call this local number: (714) 966-5600

MONDAY, OCTOBER 31, 1988 — R — Part VIII

Now at last, you can hear them too!
Mississippi Man Discovers Long Lost Tapes Made By Elvis Presley Before He Became Famous!

If you are an Elvis Presley fan, this may be the most exciting message you will ever read.

Here is why. In 1955, a full year *before* Elvis became famous, he got a chance to play at the Eagles Hall at 2204 Louisiana Street in Houston, Texas. He went there with Scotty Moore, his guitar player and first sidekick, and Bill Black, his bass player. Well, what happened is, the three of them got up there on that stage and...

THEY SET THAT JOINT ON FIRE!

You see, this was Elvis before he was tamed down, before Colonel Parker got a hold of him, before Steve Allen tried to "detwitch" him, before he was told he had to stop all that shaking or else the TV cameras could only shoot him from the waist up. *This* was Elvis *totally* uninhibited!

Well anyway, there was a DJ down in Houston named Benny Hess who used to go around recording live acts on his tape recorder and then, if he liked what he heard, he'd play the tape on his radio show. Then, after that, to save money, he'd use that same tape to record somebody else instead of saving the original recording. So, what he does this time is, he goes to the Elvis concert at the Eagles Hall and he records it and...

HE DECIDES IT'S NOT GOOD ENOUGH TO PLAY ON HIS RADIO SHOW!

Thank God! If that tape *had* been played, it would have been recorded over like all the others and, it would have been lost forever. As it turns out, however, the tape was simply tossed in a drawer where it was **forgotten for more than 20 years!**

Hard to imagine, isn't it? But, believe it or not, back then, the people at the Eagles Hall didn't even know how to spell Elvis Presley's last name. They used two S's instead of one and spelled his name "PRESSLEY." Take a look at their newspaper ad and you'll see what I mean.

> ### "...you won't believe your ears..."

Whatever. So, to get on with the story, 22-years go by and, as we all sadly remember, Elvis Presley passes away on August 16, 1977. Millions of people are plunged into depression. The King is dead and *nobody* can ever replace him.

But sometimes, even in the midst of the greatest tragedies, something good happens. And, in this case, what happens is that a man down in Mississippi (where Elvis was born) remembered that DJ who used to tape those live acts and he gets him on the phone. The man from Mississippi is a "good ol' boy" named Marcellus Allison and he asks the DJ if he ever taped Elvis. "By God, I believe I did!"

TONIGHT'S the NIGHT
From 8:00 - 11:00 P.M.

GRAND PRIZE JAMBOREE

Presents

ELVIS PRESSLEY
LOUISIANA HAYRIDE STAR

★ HOOT GIBSON
FAMOUS WESTERN MOVIE STAR
★ SONNY BURNS
★ BROWN BROS.
★ TOMMY SANDS

At Eagles' Hall
A Block South of Gray on Louisiana
with

BIFF COLLIE
as Master of Ceremonies

Also Appearing on the Show Will Be
James O'Gwynn, Coye Wilcox, the Elvis Stillman, Emis Hunter, and Hank Rochingear!

★ NEXT WEEK'S GUEST ★
TOMMY COLLINS

---

says the DJ and then, *the hunt is on!*

Well, to make a long story short, they find the tape but it is so old and so dried out it starts to crumble as soon as they touch it. So, they get a special machine that can play the tape without any tension at all and...

THEY ARE ABLE TO SAVE EVERY SINGLE SONG ELVIS SANG AT THAT CONCERT!

They also got Elvis talking to the audience between songs and, believe me, this is *not* the same Elvis you saw in all those dumb movies. No way! This is the hip-shaking, pelvis pounding, tough-talking Elvis in the first flush of his manhood before he was homogenized and "cleaned up" for public consumption!

When Scotty Moore first heard the tape, he said, "That's me, I can't deny it. You can hear Bill Black (the clown of the group) *hollering* in the background!"

So, with the help of Stan Kesler, a songwriter who was at Sun Records when Elvis was there, the tape gets converted to one side of a record album. Then, on the other side, they get Scotty Moore talking and he tells what it was like traveling around that first year with Elvis. *What stories!* Scotty tells about how he and Bill Black and Elvis got stranded in Shreveport, Louisiana *because they didn't have enough money to pay the hotel bill!* He tells about how his wife nearly ran out the back door when she first saw Elvis because he was dressed so "weirdly" in a pink suit and white shoes. He tells about their Grand Ol' Opry appearance which was a disaster. (Elvis was advised to go back to driving a truck!) He tells about how Bill Black's clowning around was needed to win the audience over so they would at least give Elvis a chance. And so on.

All in all, this may be the most historically important record album ever produced. It was tied up in lawsuits for several years but now, at last, it is available for release on a *very* limited basis to the general public.

BUT YOU MUST ACT FAST!

As you know, Elvis has sold hundreds of millions of records but this one is *truly rare*. This album is called THE FIRST YEAR and only 10,000 of this special limited edition were produced and...

THERE ARE LESS THAN 7,000 LEFT!

At only $19.95 apiece, these albums are truly a rare bargain. You see, in this case, you're not just getting a record — you're also getting a piece of history. However, because these albums are so rare...

THERE IS A STRICT LIMIT OF ONLY ONE PER CUSTOMER!

Please do not ask us to make an exception. We can't. It wouldn't be fair. There's not really enough of these albums to go around and we want to satisfy as many Elvis fans as we can with what we've got to work with.

Anyway, these albums are being sold on a first come, first-served basis with a 100% money back guarantee. They are easy to order. All you have to do is write your name and address and the words "First Elvis Album" on a piece of paper and send it with your payment of $19.95 plus $2.00 shipping and handling (total $21.95) to:

**Everett & Lloyd, Inc.
9000 Sunset Boulevard, Suite 603
Los Angeles, California 90069**

That's all there is to it. Your album will be shipped promptly (within 24 hours) as soon as we receive your order. By the way, for faster service, you can order by phone and we will send this amazing album to you C.O.D. or you can use your MasterCard, Visa or American Express. We are open from 9:00 am to 5:00 pm West Coast time and our number is...

(213) 273-7053

Either way, if you are interested, please order as soon as possible to avoid disappointment.

By the way, when you get your album, you will see that it has a reproduction of a contract signed by Elvis that also contains the *only known signature* of his mother, Gladys Presley!

In the above ad, which appeared in a 1988 issue of the Los Angeles Times, AIDA has been used effectively. The process starts with an attention grabbing headline.

Now at last, you can hear them too!

Mississippi Man Discovers Long Lost Tapes Made By Elvis Presley Before He Became Famous!

If you are an Elvis Presley fan, this may be the most exciting message you will ever read.

Here is why. In 1955, a full year *before* Elvis became famous, he got a chance to play at the Eagles Hall at 2204 Louisiana Street in Houston, Texas. He went there with Scotty Moore, his gui- says the DJ and then, *the hunt is on!*

Well, to make a long story short, they find the tape but it is so old and so dried out it starts to crumble as soon as they touch it. So, they get a special machine that can play the tape without any tension at all and...

Elvis is a public figure and it'll interest his fans to learn what he did before coming famous. By using "long lost" it adds an element of intrigue. If they've been lost for a long time then it means few people have heard it. If few people have heard it then it should be coveted.

> **THEY SET THAT JOINT ON FIRE!**
>
> You see, this was Elvis before he was tamed down, before Colonel Parker got a hold of him, before Steve Allen tried to "detwitch" him, before he was told he had to stop all that shaking or else the TV cameras could only shoot him from the waist up. *This was Elvis totally uninhibited!*
>
> Well anyway, there was a DJ down in Houston named Benny Hess who used to go around recording live acts on his tape recorder and then, if he liked what he heard, he'd play the tape on his radio show. Then, after that, to save money, he'd use that same tape to record somebody else instead of saving the original recording. So, what he does this time is, he goes to the Elvis concert at the Eagles Hall and he records it and...

They move into strong compelling paragraphs and subheadings. "Before he was tamed down." "Detwitch him." "all that shaking" "totally uninhibited". These words build a narrative about what to expect in the tapes.

If you felt like Elvis was something in his prime then you've got a lot in store for you when you listen to the tapes. After using these power words, they transition into a story. Stories are powerful.

> **THERE IS A STRICT LIMIT OF ONLY ONE PER CUSTOMER!**
>
> Please do not ask us to make an exception. We can't. It wouldn't be fair. There's <u>not really enough of these albums to go around</u> and we want to satisfy as many Elvis fans as we can with what we've got to work with.
>
> Anyway, these albums are being sold on a <u>first-come, first-served basis</u> with a 100% money back guarantee. They are easy to order. All you have to do is write your name and address and the words "First Elvis Album" on a piece of paper and send it with your payment of $19.95 plus $2.00 shipping and handling (total $21.95) to:

To build desire, they created scarcity. They let you know there's a 100% money back guarantee, but you can't buy any for your friends or family. Take a look at the language they used "not really enough of these albums to go around" and "first come, first served basis." If you're too late then sorry.

> **Everett & Lloyd, Inc.**
> **9000 Sunset Boulevard, Suite 603**
> **Los Angeles, California 90069**
>
> That's all there is to it. Your album will be shipped promptly (within 24 hours) as soon as we receive your order. By the way, for faster service, you can order by phone and we will send this amazing album to you C.O.D. or you can use your MasterCard, Visa or American Express. We are open from 9:00 am to 5:00 pm West Coast time and our number is...
>
> **(213) 273-7053**
>
> Either way, if you are interested, please order as soon as possible to avoid disappointment.
> By the way, when you get your album, you will see that it has a reproduction of a contract signed by Elvis that also contains the *only known signature* of his mother, Gladys Presley!

2 options

They allow you to get your hands on the offer in two ways. The first is a phone order with cash on delivery. The second is to mail your payment in and they'll send your goods within twenty four hours. The address is written boldly so there won't be any confusion. The number is also bold so you don't have to search for it.

The AIDA formula is as powerful as it is simple. For it to work effectively, you have to know your audience. I can't stress that fact enough. No matter how polished your writing is, you can't make a dent in your conversion rates until you know who you're talking to.

Once you have that information, you can use their language, wants, and desires to craft a thing of beauty.

The resource I want to refer you to is called The Gary Halbert Letters. He's one of the most successful copywriters to have ever lived. Just type "the Gary Halbert Letters" without the quotations and you'll see a website by the same name.

The problem is that it's horribly organized. There used to be a PDF of it floating around the internet, but it's since been taken down at the behest of his sons. I can't publish it on my website, but I can give it to you as a friend you if you shoot me an email.

Make the subject "The Gary Halber Letters" and send it to support@iaexperiment.com. You'll get a link to download the file in return.

In the next chapter, we're going to look at what you can do to maximize your thank you pages to recoup your advertising costs.

Make sure you get the worksheets that come with a checklist, swipe file, and headline formulas. https://www.iaexperiment.com/landing-worksheets

Chapter Nine: Making Money with Thank you Pages

There's a harsh reality when it comes to business. If you're not making money then you're losing it. You spend money on overhead such as hosting, software, and staff. You're lucky if you don't have to stock inventory and other physical assets.

You have other expenses such as your ISP, paper, and advertising costs. Let's not get into services providers like designers, marketers, and content creators. Some of your landing pages won't be able to provide an instant ROI.

They're not built for that, they're built to generate leads through downloads, Ebooks, and free trials. Your funnel may be long or short. I don't know, it's different for every business. I know some of mine are thirty days or more.

What does that mean?

It means I'm not going to make a tangible amount of money from a lead until about thirty days have passed. That could be a problem when I have to continually shell out cash to keep my business running.

In this chapter, I'm going to take advantage of a method that surprisingly few people use to offset their advertising costs. It delivers something relevant and valuable to your subscribers and keeps you afloat while you get your backend to do its job.

There's a reason why the strategy I'm going to present in this chapter is so damn effective. When people subscribe to your mailing list, they're more engaged with you than they'll ever be again. Think about it. How do you interact with a new person or company in your inbox?

You open their first few emails to decide if they're worth listening to. If they're not, you tune them out or unsubscribe and move on with your life. This is a unique opportunity for you, the entrepreneur, to instantly turn them into a customer while engagement is at its highest.

I'm not going to get into what you should email them for the next few days and weeks. What I'm referring to comes before all of that. I'm talking about how to use your thank you page and possibly the first few emails as a way to offset the cost of lead generation.

The Thank You Page
Thank you pages are a necessary part of lead generation and sales. It's the next step after your visitor has completed one of your desired actions. It could be a webinar registration, a resource download, or a purchase. They let your visitors know you appreciate their time, attention, and money. It's also an opportunity for you to tell them what to do next.

When used correctly, they reduce anxiety and promote a positive user experience. When used incorrectly, they leave a sour taste in your visitor's mouth.

In the best case scenario, you turn them into an advocate and get them to perform another desired action. Let's look at a few of the basic building blocks of an optimized thank you page. After that, I'll show you how to optimize yours for revenue.

1. *Confirm the action:*
The first step you take on the thank you page is to confirm your visitor's conversion. This is could be as simple as saying "Thank you for signing up for the dog training 101 webinar". In reality, it should never be more complicated than that.

It serves as a way to make sure everyone is on the same page. If it was a paid offer, your best bet is to be specific. If it's a lead magnet, you can get away with a general thank you page.

Create a thank you page template and save it. Any time you're creating a new landing page, switch out the text to reflect confirmation of your offer and you'll be good to go.

Simply measured confirms exactly what you opted in for. They also give you a few instructions to make sure you're able to get your hands on it.

2. Add social buttons

Right after a conversion, your visitors will be more engaged with your brand than ever. Use this opportunity to add social buttons so they can become part of your ecosystem. There are two ways to do this.

1. Just add the buttons and hope they'll understand what you want.
2. Add a clear prompt about why they should follow you on social media.

The second option is better because it shows you're not taking their time and attention for granted.

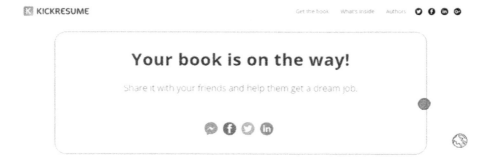

3. Ask your visitor to share

It may seem obvious but it's not. You always have a higher chance of success when you ask for the action. Don't assume that people will love your offer and share it with the world. Even if they love it, the thought may not cross their minds.

Ask them for it and you may be pleasantly surprised at how much traffic you're able to generate because of it.

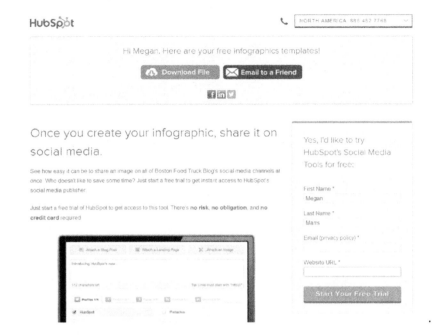

Hubspot is doing a lot of things well on their thank you page. They confirm the specific offer and also make it easy to share. They also prompt their visitors to sign up for a free trial of their software.

4. Social proof

You can never have enough social proof. Even though the person on your thank you page has already performed your desired action, it won't hurt to let them know they're not alone. A simple way to get the desired effect is through testimonials or dropping a few big numbers.

Add the number of people who've already downloaded the resource or a glowing review. You're opening the door to further positive actions down the line.

"Huge fan. I've used many apps before but Sprout has some of the best reporting for teams using social media I have found."

KOKA SEXTON
Director of Social Media Strategy

These are the basic building blocks of high impact thank you pages, but they won't earn revenue immediately. Everything is geared towards a positive user experience and increased awareness.

To take your thank you page a step further, there's something called a front end offer you'll take advantage of.

A front end offer is a valuable yet inexpensive product or service you offer visitors in order to shift the dynamic from casual observer to customer. Before we continue, I want to differentiate between a tripwire offer and a front end offer.

A tripwire offer is a product or service priced extremely low. It's usually sub ten dollars. When I refer to a front end offer, I'm talking about products priced between twenty and thirty dollars. They're generally less than forty dollars.

Why does it matter? It's all about perception.

If you price yourself too low, depending on the product, it can have negative repercussions on your brand. When you make it a price war instead of a battle on value then it's a race to the bottom. No one wins.

Moving on.

The point of the front end offer on your thank you page or anywhere for that matter is to acquire as many customers as possible at a breakeven point. It pays for all your acquisition expenses. Everything else you sell to that customer is profit for your business.

The key to making this work is creating products that go above and beyond the expectations of the new customer. That way, they'll be eager to continue doing business with you.

Don't fall into the trap of creating worthless front end products. People may not go through the trouble of asking for a refund, but they definitely won't buy from you again.

A front end offer should:

1. Be of top notch quality
2. Deliver more than what you promised
3. Create an amazing experience
4. Push them further down your funnel.

When it's on your thank you page, there's another criteria that needs to be filled. The offer should be relevant to what they just opted into. If they just got an Ebook on content marketing, a content calendar would be a great offer.

Now, let's look at a few examples of offers on thank you pages.

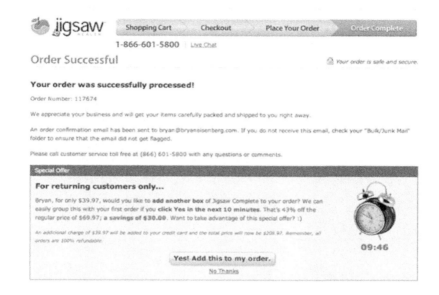

Jigsaw Health is a premium dietary supplement manufacturer. After you've opted in or purchased something they follow thank you page best practices by confirming your order.

They take it a step further and display deeply discounted limited time offers. They state what you're getting and then show you a timer in the bottom right corner of your screen. In addition to the timer, they highlight the savings amount in (43%) in red text. There's no way you're missing it.

The page above plays to a psychological phenomenon known as loss aversion. We fight harder to keep something (in this case it's a discount) than we do to gain something new. Remember I told you about human greed in Chapter Four? It's still alive and well.

131

I love this thank you page by Spanish Pod 101. At the top of the page they have a video that says thank you in 29 different languages. When I saw it, I was intrigued.

Even though I wasn't too interested in signing up for a premium package, I was curious and decided to scroll down the page. They offer a 30% discount on their packages for signing up. The clearly listed benefits are a plus.

No matter what you say about him as a president, Barack Obama used digital marketing strategies well. He had the largest war chest in presidential history. Part of that was a great thank you page.

When people signed up to get more information or just stay in the loop. They were presented with a number of options. One of which was donating to the cause.

They added social proof by stating 1,700,000 people had already donated. All those people couldn't be wrong could they? They also asked people to register to vote and volunteer. Even if they didn't generate income directly, they were still moving towards their ultimate goal of putting Obama in the White House.

Amazon is the largest internet retailer in the world. They also know how to use their thank you pages effectively.

Amazon confirms your order and gets the fine print out of the way. They use a combination of social proof and your browsing habits to recommend more products for you.

Remember, your visitor is never more engaged with you than the moments after they complete your desired action. Use it to your advantage with your thank you pages.

An advanced strategy which I'll just mention here is stacking offers. For example, if your prospect opts into your front end offer, you can instantly transition to one of your core offers.

The key here is to make sure it's relevant.

Your landing pages are the beginning of a process to give your prospects what they need. Use them in conjunction with relevant offers to essentially build a database of customers for free.

Final thoughts on Building Irresistible Landing Pages

You've given me something precious. Your time. Thank you for that. I've done the best I could to make it worthwhile and hope that was reflected in the content of this book.

Now it's your turn.

Landing pages are essential when it comes to generating leads and revenue for your business. You can either throw up whatever comes to mind or you can follow a systematic approach as outlined in this book.

Either way, you'll get results. They're the results you want or results you don't.

Your journey is your own. Since you've gotten this far, I'm happy that I was able to be a part of it for the few minutes or hours it took you to read this book.

The worst thing you can do is fail to implement any of the insights you've gained while reading it. We're all guilty of reading a book, promising to make changes, then failing to follow through. I understand. I've been there and I've done that.

There's no time like the present to make an effective change. You've got to start somewhere right?

Though this book is about landing pages, your business is more than the sum of the properties you build. It's more than twenty high converting landing pages. It's an entity that delivers value to everyone that interacts with it.

Value comes through in the quality of products and services you put out into the world. Your story is what makes people give you a chance in the first place.

If your story isn't compelling then no matter what bells and whistles you attach to it, you won't see any progress.

They don't care about the latest and greatest product you're producing.

They don't care about the thousand shares your most recent post got.

They don't care about how many comments your posts get.

What they care about is how you make them feel and the problems you can solve.

Whether they become customers or not is irrelevant. You have a mission and a story. Landing pages are a vehicle to tell that story and advance your mission to every corner of the globe. To be a standout success, you need to hold that mission front and center.

Always challenge yourself more than you did yesterday. We can only go in two directions – forward or backward. I know you don't want to go backward. There's nothing for you there. The landing pages you build over the next few days, weeks, months, and years are meant to take you forward.

This book is comprehensive. I'll argue with anyone that says it isn't. At the same time, it's just a starting point. I could never tell you everything you'll ever need to know.

The secret to always staying in front of the curve is to test. Test everything you've read in this book. If you don't like one of the rules I laid out, break it until you find something better. When you do, shoot me an email. I'll be more than happy to implement what you've discovered.

And remember, no man is an island entire unto himself.

To get featured across our network of pages, retweeted, or mentioned take a picture of your book with the following hashtags. Or, use the hashtags to give me a shout and let me know you're enjoying it.

#landingpageboss

#LikeABoss

#LikeABossSeries

#TheXPLife

#XPNation

Landing Page Checklist

Landing Page Swipefile

Headline Formulas

Urgent Plea!

Thank you for Reading my Book!

I really appreciate your feedback and love hearing what you have to say. In fact, all the updates I make for my books are as a direct result of reader feedback.

That means I need your feedback to make the next version better.

Please leave a helpful review on Amazon telling me whether you hated it or (hopefully) loved it.

Thanks so much.

Daniel Ndukwu

Printed in Great Britain
by Amazon